Alteryx™ For Accounting, Tax and Finance Professionals

by
Trent Green

TAX
DIRECTOR
SERVICES

ALTERYX FOR ACCOUNTING, TAX AND FINANCE PROFESSIONALS

ISBN: 9798578651236
Imprint: Independently published

For information, contact:
Tax Director Services
1273 Horsham Way
Apex, NC 27502

www.nctaxdirector.com

Table of Contents

1 Preliminary Matters

1.1 About Me

I am an author, continuing professional education (CPE) developer, instructor, conference speaker, and Fortune 500 corporate tax contractor and consultant through my company, Tax Director Services (www.nctaxdirector.com).

Before starting Tax Director Services, I was the Head of Tax for PROS, a $160M publicly traded company. Before joining PROS, I was a Tax Director with PwC. Prior to that, I oversaw international tax for SAS, a $2.7 billion multinational software corporation operating in more than 50 countries.

I began my career in public accounting with Coopers & Lybrand (which became PwC) working on a variety of corporate, partnership, and individual income tax issues. I have a Bachelor of Arts, a Business Minor, and Master of Accounting degrees from UNC-Chapel Hill. I have taught CPE and done conference presentations since 2009, and in 2016 I received a "5.0 Speaker Award" from the North Carolina Association of CPAs. Finally, I have extensive experience working with youth through The Church of Jesus Christ of Latter-day Saints, coaching baseball, and community service. I live with my family in Apex, North Carolina.

My full professional profile is at www.linkedin.com/in/trentgreen.

1.2 Other Books

- "The Missing Tax Accounting Guide – A Plain English Introduction to ASC 740."
- "Tax Department Productivity: People, Processes and Technology."[1]

1.3 Copyright Information

No part of this material has been authorized for free download, transmission, or any form of copying (paper or electronic) by professionals, firms, students, or any other person or organization. Further, this material may not be used to teach continuing or professional education courses without the express written permission of the author.

1.4 Trademarked Terms

- All references to "Alteryx" or "Designer" refer to Alteryx Designer™, a software product created and maintained by Alteryx, Inc.

---

[1] This is designed for use as a CPE course manual and was not written to be a standalone book.

- All references to "Excel" refer to Microsoft Excel™, a software product created and maintained by Microsoft Corporation.

1.5   Legal Disclaimer

This material is sold with the understanding it does not constitute accounting, tax or legal services or advice.

1.6   The Focus of the Material in this Book

The focus of this material is on the use of Alteryx for accounting, tax, and finance professionals. Alteryx has many capabilities that go beyond the scope of this material. I purposefully avoid these additional features and functions to keep this material concise and relevant.

1.7   Investment Disclosure[2]

I became an investor in Alteryx in April of 2021.

As additional background, after becoming an Alteryx user I achieved significantly higher levels of productivity when working with large datasets. I subsequently wrote this book because of my love of technical writing and my excitement to share what I had learned with my fellow professionals. It was only after writing the first draft of this book that I became an investor in Alteryx. I did so because I believed from hands-on Fortune 500 experience that it would have a growing and lasting impact on accounting, tax, and finance professionals.

Knowing that I have a personal stake in the success of Alteryx as a company, I invite you to read this book and the positive things I have to say about the software with all the skepticism you wish to bring. For the record, I want you to know that I believe everything I that I have written within these covers, both the good and the bad, and I now leave it to you to make your own fully informed judgment.

1.8   NASBA Compliant Alteryx CPE

If you would like to enroll in NASBA compliant CPE I've produced on Alteryx, then see:

- www.nctaxdirector.com/courses or
- taxdirectorservices.advancecpe.com.

---

[2] I am not an employee of Alteryx. Everything I say about Alteryx and its software is my own opinion and does not represent the official views of the company.

2 An Introduction to Alteryx Terminology and Concepts

2.1 Learning Objectives

Upon the completion of this chapter, you will be able to:

- Understand the meaning of specific terms related to Alteryx.
- Articulate the complementary strengths of Alteryx and Excel for CPAs.
- Identify the areas of Alteryx's main screen, as well as each area's purpose and function.
- Understand the concept of an Alteryx "workflow," as well as the optimal approach for designing and testing workflows.
- Know how to get self-help withing the Alteryx Designer program.
- Know how to access additional training and resources through the online "Alteryx Community."
- Maximize the use of your time to effort in learning Alteryx in ways that are most impactful for CPAs.

2.2 "Alteryx Designer"

Before we dive into technical material, let's get some Alteryx-related terminology straight.

The company

- "Alteryx" is the name of a U.S.-based software company.[3]

The software

- Alteryx makes "Alteryx Designer," the software program that's the subject of this material.

The abbreviated name of the software

- Alteryx Designer is frequently referred to as:
    - "Alteryx" or
    - "Designer."

---

[3] "Alteryx is a leader in analytic process automation (APA). Its APA platform unifies analytics, data science and business process automation in one, end-to-end platform to accelerate digital transformation." – From the company's November 2020 press kit at https://www.alteryx.com.

o   These same abbreviated naming conventions are used throughout this material (i.e., "Alteryx" or "Designer," referring to the software).

2.3   Comparing the Complementary Strengths of Alteryx and Excel

The strengths of Excel

- Excel is an outstanding tool for:
    o   Quick calculations.
    o   Customized, freehand worksheets and workbooks.

The strengths of Alteryx

- From an accounting, tax, and finance point of view, Alteryx is best for:
    o   Organizing, formatting, and cleaning data so that it can be more readily used in Excel calculations.
    o   Handling recurring and repetitive data-related tasks ("process automation").
    o   Analyzing and manipulating large datasets that would require a substantial amount of manual work if done using Excel on a standalone basis.

Alteryx's fit among CPA software tools

- Think of Alteryx as an ADDITION to (and NOT as a *replacement* for) Excel.

- Key points:
    o   I'm not biased towards Excel or Alteryx.
    o   I do not view one as "better" than the other.
    o   They're both tools with different strengths that serve specific needs.

Analogies for comparing Alteryx with Excel

1) Favoring Excel over Alteryx would be like saying a hammer is better than a screwdriver.
    a. A hammer and a screwdriver both perform useful functions; one is not better than another.
    b. The point: Use the right tool for the job.
    c. It's unproductive to try and use one tool for everything.
        i. Would you hammer a nail with a screwdriver?

2) Select the right golf club depending on your shot.
    a. Just because a driver works great off the tee doesn't mean it's the right club to use in a sand trap.
    b. A putter wouldn't be good in either case, but it's vastly superior to all other clubs on the putting green.

    c.   The point: You have multiple clubs in your golf bag for a reason; they all serve important purposes.

Bottom line: Excel and Alteryx are BOTH valuable tools for accounting, tax, and finance professionals.

2.4   An Explanation of Areas on Alteryx's Main Screen

There's an artistic theme that plays into the naming of the various areas of Designer's main screen.

The Tool Palette

- The Tool Palette is at the top of the screen.
- It contains the full library of Alteryx tools that are used to work with your data.
- A portion of the "Favorites" section of the Tool Palette is pictured below

| Browse | Input Data | Output Data | Text Input | Data Cleansing | Filter | Formula | Sample | Select | Select Records |

The Canvas

- The Canvas is in the middle of the screen (it says, "Drop tools here," as shown below).

- This is where you drag tools from the Tool Palette to create workflows (the middle).
  - The concept of "workflows" will be explained shortly.

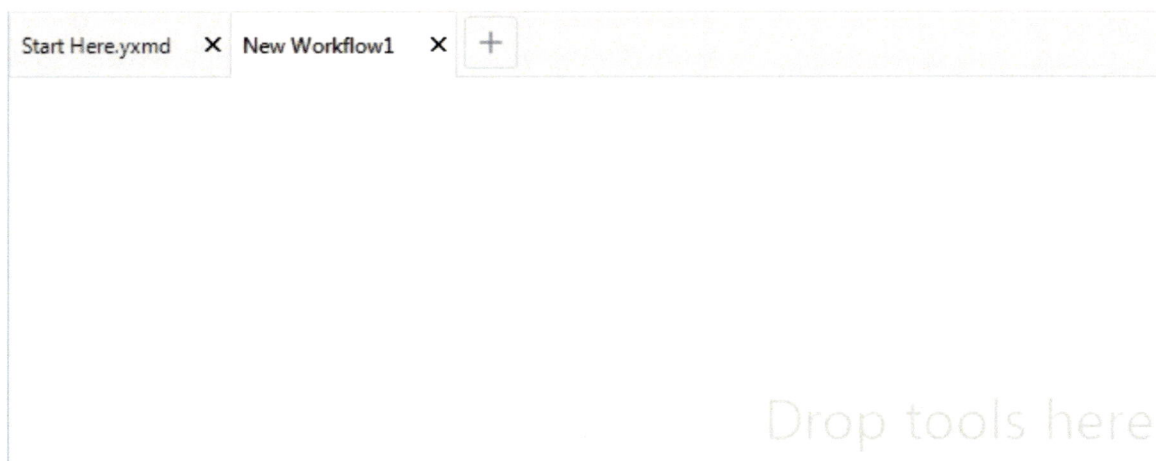

Start Here.yxmd   ✕   New Workflow1   ✕   +

Drop tools here

The Configuration Window

- After you drag a tool to the Canvas, you need to configure it to interact with your data the way you intend.

- You configure a tool by clicking on it. After doing so, options for the tool will appear in the Configuration Window on the left side of the screen.

- It's here that you customize Alteryx tools to meet your needs.
  - This is one of the best features of Alteryx, to be able to customize data analysis with visual tools and menus rather than having to learn software code.

- Each tool has a different configuration, and I will walk you through many of them as we progress through the material.
  - The configuration below is what you see when there are NO tools on the Canvas.
    - You can use this configuration to control various ways in which Alteryx works.
    - For information, in working on accounting, tax and finance issues, I have not found it necessary to adjust this standard configuration.

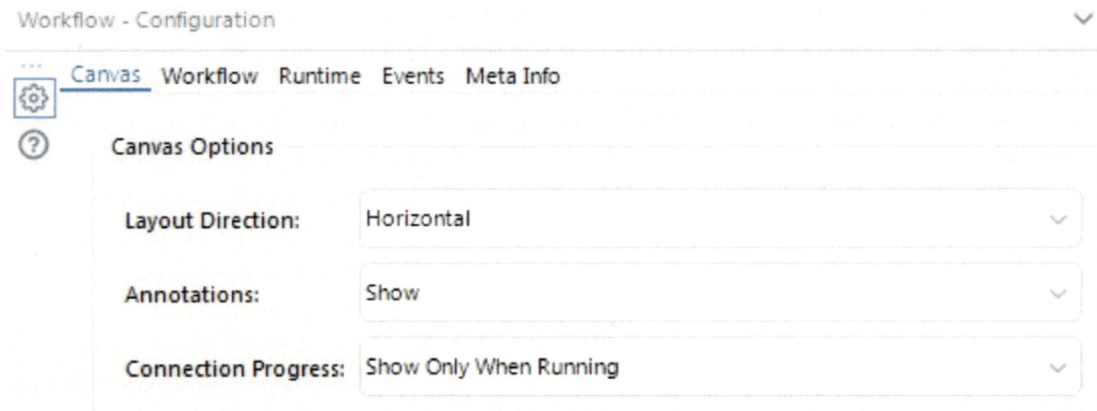

Workflow - Configuration

Canvas   Workflow   Runtime   Events   Meta Info

Canvas Options

Layout Direction:	Horizontal
Annotations:	Show
Connection Progress:	Show Only When Running

Results Window

- The Results Window is at the bottom of the screen, below the Canvas.

- This is where you see the results of your data analysis, or your "workflow."
  - Again, I will explain the "workflow" concept shortly.

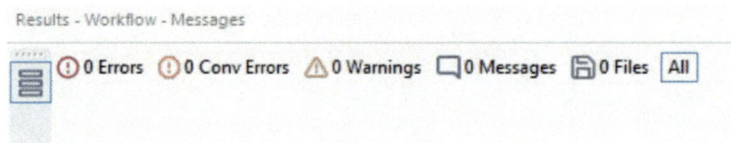

Results - Workflow - Messages

0 Errors   0 Conv Errors   0 Warnings   0 Messages   0 Files   All

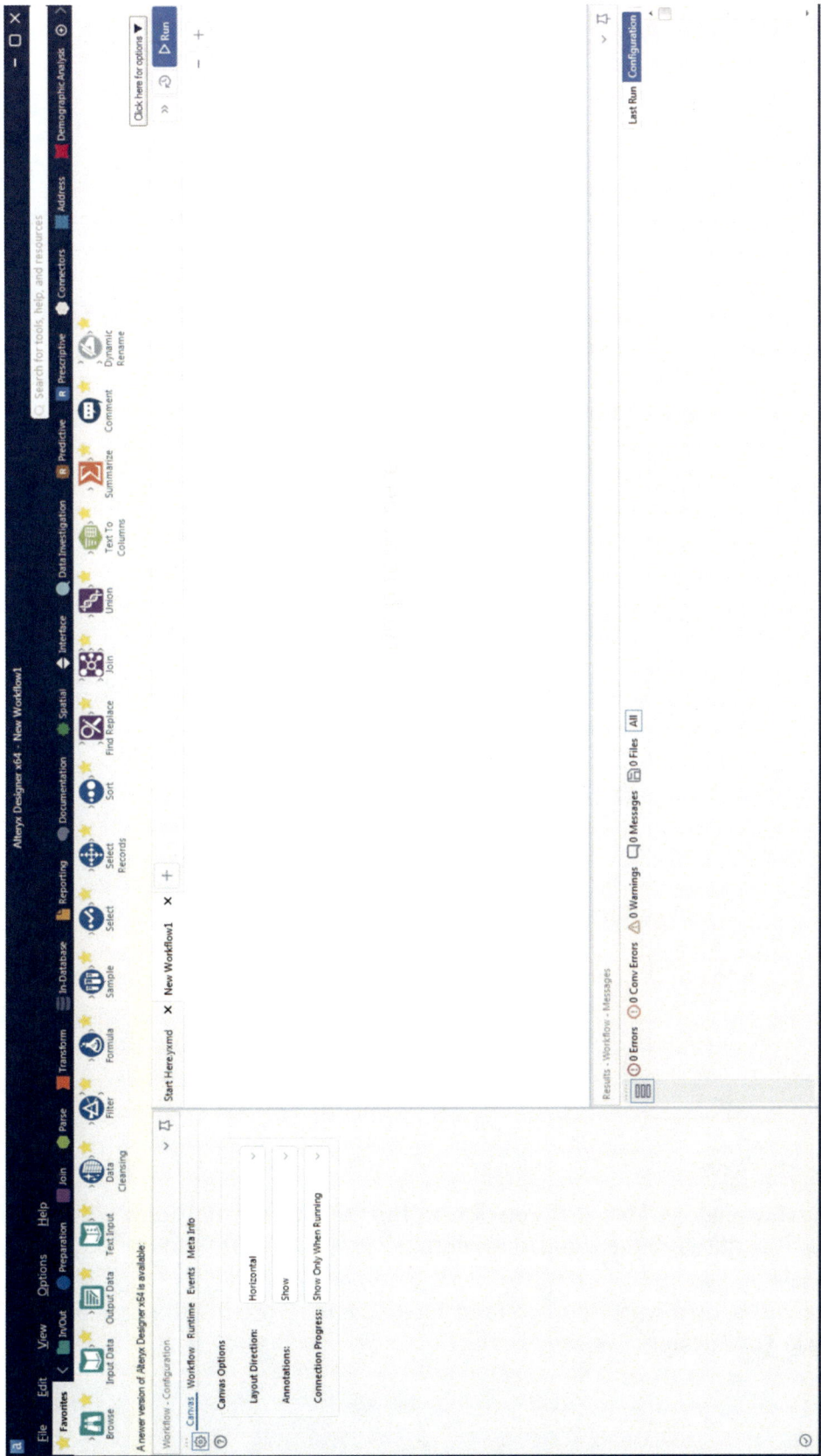

2.5   An Introduction to The Workflow Concept

The basics

- A "workflow" is a key concept in Alteryx.

- Think of a workflow as a stream of data that starts at the left of the screen and moves (or "flows") to the right until it comes to the end.

- A workflow is made up of Alteryx tools that you drag to the Canvas from the Tool Palette. In other words, data "flows" from one tool to another.

The process of designing a workflow

- A workflow will almost always start with an "Input Data" tool because that's what brings your data (e.g., an Excel file) into the Alteryx Designer software program.
    - o I will cover the "Input Data" tool in more detail in the next chapter.

- From there, you will add other tools to the Canvas depending on what you need to do to organize, format, cleanse, manipulate, and analyze your data.

- It's important to note that as you are dragging various tools to the Canvas and configuring them, *nothing is happening to your source data*.
    - o Said another way, your source file is not deleted, modified, or changed in any way as you work with the data it contains within Alteryx.

- Think of designing a workflow like building a canal.
    - o As a farmer, a river has the potential to be incredibly useful in watering crops, but it won't happen automatically; you have to be intentional about diverting water to your crops.
    - o As you begin to build a canal for this purpose, there is no water is passing through it.
    - o Your goal at this opening stage is to create a channel to take water from where it is (a nearby river) and guide it to where you want it to go (to water the crops on your property).

Running your workflow

- Continuing with the analogy above, if you never "flip the switch," no water will ever travel from the river, through the canal, and on to the crops in your field.

- Similarly, once you build a workflow, you must activate it before it will process your data according to your design.

- You activate a workflow by clicking on the "Run" button in the top-right of the Canvas. When you do this, the following steps occur:
  - Your data is imported into Alteryx through an "Input Data" tool.
  - From there, it travels from left to right, progressively "flowing" through the tools you incorporated into the workflow.
  - As part of this process, your data is organized, formatted, cleansed, manipulated, and analyzed according to how you ordered and configured the tools in the workflow.

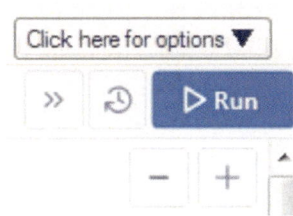

- After the workflow has run (meaning your data has run through all the tools), you will hear a chime letting you know that it processed correctly.
  - You will hear a dissonant "clang" sound if there is an error in your workflow.
  - We will talk about what errors mean and how to deal with them as we progress through the material.

- After your workflow runs, the Results Window below the Canvas will be populated with your output. By reviewing it, you can get a sense of whether the workflow transformed, calculated, or otherwise impacted your data according to expectations.

2.6   Test your Workflow as You're Building It

Revisiting the "canal" analogy

- Let's assume you've now spent a substantial amount of time to build your canal from start to finish to direct water to your crops, which are two miles away.

- However, when you flip the switch to let water flow from the river into the canal, momentum causes it to leap over the sides of the channel after traveling just a few hundred feet.
  - In short, despite all your efforts, the disappointing outcome is that your canal didn't divert water from the river as intended, and you're now going to have to invest even more time to fix it.

- There is a better way. Rather than waiting unto the very end of the process to test your canal, you can let the water pass through it on a periodic basis to ensure that it's flowing as expected.
  - If it's not, you can address the problem right away and then continue from there.

- Following this pattern, you can consistently and methodically progress towards your goal (watering your crops), saving yourself a significant amount of time, effort, and grief along the way.

The dangers of NOT testing your workflow

- Following the analogy above, clicking "Run" is what sends a "stream" of data through your Alteryx workflow.

- Exaggerating to make a point, let's say that you have 100 tools in your workflow, and you don't click "Run" for the first time until the very end.

- Unfortunately, in this example, it's obvious from previewing the Results Window that your final output isn't anything remotely close to what you need or expected.

- This means you've now got a messy, complex problem on your hands.
    - Which tool is creating the problem?
    - Is it one of the first ones (tool #4), or was everything okay until the data got near the end (tool #99)?
    - Worse still, what if the problem lies with _multiple_ tools that aren't configured properly?

- To summarize, if you don't test your workflow until the very end, you'll have no way of knowing where your workflow came off the rails without going through the tedious process of reviewing each tool's configurations starting at the beginning and working through to the end.
    - To make matters worse, you may find along the way (say after you review tool #34) that you need to design the workflow in an entirely different manner to address the issue (meaning you wasted time configuring tools 35 through 100!).

"Run as you go"

- As I noted before, there is a better, more efficient, more sanity-preserving way to develop your workflows, which I refer to as "Run as you go."

- Every time you drag a tool to the Canvas, you're effectively asking it to do something to your data.

- Is this happening? Is a tool performing as you intended? All you have to do to confirm this is to "cut on the water" by clicking "Run."

- After doing so, your data will flow through each tool. You can then check the Results Window to ensure the output is what you expected.
    - If everything looks good, add the next tool to the workflow, configure it, repeat the testing process, adjust as needed, and continue from there.

- If your workflow isn't working as intended, carefully evaluate the data output displaying in the Results Window.
    - How is it different than what you expected?
    - Did you use the right tool?
    - If so, is the tool configured properly?
    - Do you need to change your overall approach in developing the workflow, using a combination of different tools and configurations to accomplish your objectives?

Bottom Line: Whatever the problem with your workflow may be, it's a LOT easier to address it as you go vs. trying to identify and fix it later after it's deeply embedded in a complex web of tools.

Testing workflows with large datasets

- "Running as you go" works fine with smaller datasets.
    - For example, your workflow will normally process in just a few seconds if there are only a few hundred lines in your data.

- However, workflow processing will slow *substantially* if you're dealing with larger datasets (i.e., thousands, tens of thousands, or even hundreds of thousands of lines of data).
    - There are also certain tools that can slow down workflow processing.

- Such processing delays can cause it to be very tedious to test your workflow by running it.

- As a workaround, you can *design* your workflow using a smaller portion of your source data.

- For example:
    - Let's say you have 100,000 lines of sales data that you want to analyze.
    - You notice that, despite the volume, the data is uniform in its presentation.
    - That being the case, you create a separate data file (housed in an Excel spreadsheet, for example) that contains only 1,000 lines of the sales data.
    - You use this smaller Excel file to design and test your workflow.
    - After the workflow is processing the test sales data exactly how you want, you can then connect it to the full dataset with 100,000 lines.

- While the above workaround will work, we'll see in the next chapter on the "Input Data" tool that there's an even more efficient way to manage the data that comes into your workflow.

2.7 Getting Self-Help within Alteryx Designer

Right-click on a tool

- To get help on a tool within Designer, right-click on it while it's still in the Tool Palette.

- Select "Help" to read a description of what the tool does and how to configure it.

- Select "Open Example" to see examples for how the how the tool works in different situations and scenarios.
  - I *really like* this section because the examples are set up as live workflows that you can run, evaluate, analyze, reconfigure, and test in a hands-on manner.

"Search for tools, help and resources"

- There is a search box in the top-right of the Alteryx screen where you can type a description of what you're looking for or trying to accomplish.

> Search for tools, help, and resources

- The search feature on some websites is second-rate, but I've found this one to be very good in terms of bringing up relevant information, examples, commentary, etc.

2.8 The "Alteryx Community:" Online Learning, Help and Networking

The "Community"

- If you license Alteryx, then you're also eligible to join "The Alteryx Community" (or "the Community" website for short).
  - The website is at:
    - community.alteryx.com
  - Note that alteryx.com is the corporate website and is NOT where to go for technical help.

- Following are ways you can learn more about Alteryx, workflows, use cases, and so forth within the Community.

The "Academy"

- The "Academy" for Alteryx is located on the toolbar at the left-hand side of the Community website. Here you can access:
  - o Interactive lessons and
  - o Weekly challenges.

"Interactive Lessons" – How they are organized

- The interactive training lessons in this section run from roughly five to fifteen minutes in length depending on the topic and the complexity of the subject matter.

- You could go through "all" of the training sessions, but this would be unproductive for accounting, tax, and finance professionals because there are many modules that cover features you would never use.

- Fortunately, the modules are categorized in logical groupings so you can focus on training that's the best fit for your needs.

- A good place to begin is the "Getting Started" section. If that training works for you then I also recommend the sections:
  - o "Alteryx for Excel Users,"
  - o "Writing Expressions," and possibly
  - o "Parsing Data."

My View of the "Interactive Lessons"

- Overall, I like the "Interactive Lessons" because, beginning with the "Getting Started" section, they provide a logical way to progressively learn Alteryx without getting tossed into a workflow and having to figure everything out on the fly.

- I also like the lessons because they present material without me having to think of questions.
  - o Said another way, how can I know what questions to ask about Alteryx when I don't even know its capabilities or how it works?
  - o In other words, the lessons provide summaries that help answer the questions "What can I do with Alteryx?" and "How do I get there?"

- While I think the lessons are helpful, I also think there are areas where they fall short.

- For example, the lessons explain how Alteryx is used in what I would call an "animated," narrative-type of format.
  - o In other words, the lessons don't do a good job showing how Alteryx is used in practice.
  - o Instead, you're presented with a blend of Alteryx screenshots coupled with animated data moving artistically around the screen.

- I would much rather see and listen to someone walk through examples using real data with visuals and screenshots of Designer and less emphasis on artistic animation of geometric objects.

- What this meant for me as I was learning Alteryx was:
  - I often had to watch a "5 minute" lesson two or three times to process what was being presented.
  - From there, it took even more time (and often a LOT more time) to apply what I had been taught in ways that would actually help me on the job.

- In summary, while the interactive lessons were an important part of helping me to "get there" as far as understanding how to use Alteryx, as a busy tax professional I sometimes found myself frustrated with the time I had to invest to do so.[4]

The Alteryx "Weekly Challenge"

- The "Weekly Challenge" is one of the selections in the "Academy" section of the Alteryx Community website.

- The idea behind the weekly challenge is to present a "real world" data-related problem and to use Alteryx tools to solve it.

My View of the "Weekly Challenge"

- I love the *idea* behind the weekly challenge.

- The interactive lessons described above and resources such as this book equip you with Alteryx-related knowledge and skills, and the weekly challenge is a way to see if you've learned enough to solve actual problems.

- Expanding on the previous point, I appreciate the challenges that are business-related, and specifically those that are geared towards accounting and finance professionals.
  - Corporate tax is never given a spotlight in the challenges, ostensibly because it's too narrow a specialization.
  - It could also be because corporate tax is considered too boring! ☺

- I also appreciate challenges that deal how to organize and manipulate large datasets, because there are many accounting and finance-related applications for this.

- However, in my estimation, most of the weekly challenges don't fall into the above categories. Instead, many are about things such as:

---

[4] This last point is one of the reasons that I decided to write this book – to help accounting, tax and finance professionals more quickly learn the Alteryx tools and methods they need to succeed while not wasting time on features, tools, and capabilities, that aren't relevant for our field of work.

- Calculating the optimal number of reindeer that should pull Santa's sleigh.
- How to solve a certain kind of puzzle.
- How to optimize flower arrangements (I'm serious…challenge #213), and so on.[5]

- In summary, as an accounting, tax or finance professional, there is a danger that you can spin your wheels on weekly challenges that will never remotely resemble anything you will encounter on the job.
  - As a result, be discriminating about what challenges you work on if you choose to tackle some as part of your learning.

Alteryx Certification

- According to Alteryx's website, "The Alteryx Certification Program…allows you to:
  - Demonstrate your proficiency across Alteryx products and versions.
  - To communicate your expertise in a standardized manner and to
  - Promote your personal brand in the global Alteryx community and marketplace."[6]

- Based on the above, should you seek to become Alteryx certified?

- In my opinion, if you need to be Alteryx certified to get the job that you want or it's necessary to separate you from the competition then I believe the answer is yes.

- Also, if you need to learn Alteryx but lack motivation (which is doubtful if you're reading this book), pursuing the Alteryx certification could be helpful if it "forces" you to learn it.

- Barring the above, I don't see a need for accounting and tax professionals to become Alteryx certified.
  - Accounting and tax professionals are most often hired based on other sets of skills and experience.
    - For now, an Alteryx certification is a "nice to have" and not a "must have" to qualify for most tax and accounting positions.
      - Demonstrating proficiency and practical experience with Alteryx would be attractive to most prospective employers even without the certification.

---

[5] I think the theory on the part of those running the Alteryx Community is if I solve the "Santa" challenge then I'll be able to take that knowledge and apply it to "something else that's truly relevant." Instead of this approach, I would like to see fewer "fluffy stuff" challenges and more that focus directly on the "something else that's truly relevant."
[6] See https://community.alteryx.com/t5/Analytics/Announcing-the-Alteryx-Product-Certification-Program/ba-p/80136.

- In addition, becoming Alteryx certified would entail accounting and tax professionals having to learn a lot of Alteryx tools and features that they would never use on the job, which is a waste of time.

- For finance professionals (as being distinct from accounting and tax professionals), the answer to whether you should become Alteryx certified varies depending on what area you're in and how in demand your skills are, but the general principles outlined above still apply.

"Search the Community"

- Sometimes you'll have a question about something you've never encountered, or the answer exists but you don't know where to find it in this book or the resources previously outlined.

- For ad hoc questions that fall into this category, the "Search the Community" bar on the "Community" home page is an excellent resource.
  - As previously noted, there are some really "dumb" search engines within websites and software programs that don't ever seem to ever produce anything useful.
  - That said, I've been pleased with Alteryx's search engine for its ability to surface relevant information.

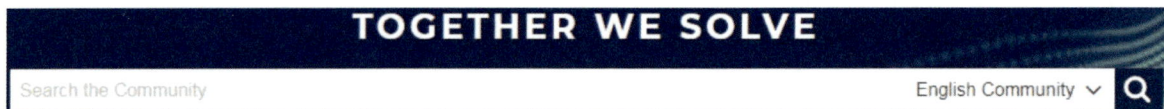

TOGETHER WE SOLVE

Search the Community   English Community ∨ 🔍

"Ask a Question"

- In addition to being able to search, access to the Alteryx Community enables you to ask a specific question.

ASK A QUESTION ►

- In Cyberspace, such a question might simply hang out there, eternally remaining unanswered.

- However, Alteryx employees as well as rabidly enthusiastic members of the user community prowl around the message boards, so you're very likely to get a timely answer to most questions.

- The ability to ask questions and to <u>get answers on your specific issues</u> is one of the best and most powerful benefits of the Community.

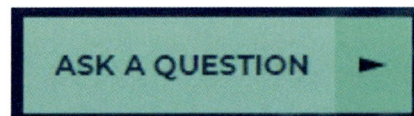

- As a matter of etiquette, you should first type your question in the "Search the Community" section to ensure the answer is not right in front of your face before asking the Community for help.
    - o This doesn't mean you need to be paranoid; people will give you a mulligan if you ask a "dumb" or "obvious" question now and then.
    - o However, it's bad form to repeatedly ask questions that you can find on your own with a little effort using available resources.

3 Getting Started – Importing Data into Your Workflow

3.1 Learning Objectives

Upon the completion of this chapter, you will:

- Learn how to import data into an Alteryx workflow using an "Input Data" tool, including effective shortcuts for doing so.
- Identify data types and formats aside from Excel files that can be imported into Alteryx, and how this contrasts with an Excel-based approach.
- Understand how Alteryx preserves your source data as you make modifications to it using tools in your workflow.
- Recognize why Alteryx's design is a natural fit for strengthening SOX controls.
- Be able to apply nuances of the "Input Data" tool to take charge of how imported data appears in your workflow.
- Learn how to limit the records read into Alteryx during the workflow design phase to speed testing using the "run as you go" approach.

3.2 "Input Data" – Import Data into a Workflow

Importing data is always the first step

- Nothing happens in Alteryx until you import data into the program.

- Once you do, you can use Alteryx tools to work with your data in ways that accomplish your goals.

- The "Input Data" tool allows you to import data from external sources and files into to your workflow.

Input Data

- As a result, for all practical purposes, the "Input Data" tool is almost always the tool that's at the beginning of a workflow.

Common data files to import

- Excel files are the most common data source to import into Alteryx for accounting, tax, and finance professionals.

- Other common data source file types to import into workflows using an "Input Data" tool include:

- o .csv - Comma separated value.
- o .xml – Extensible markup language.
- o .text – Text files

- The bottom line is if there is if a software program stores data, there is a high likelihood that you can find a way to import it into Alteryx.

- That said, PDF files are noticeably absent from the list.
  - o To my knowledge, the standard version of Designer does not read PDF files.

Source data imported into Alteryx remains unchanged

- As noted in Chapter 2, a workflow does NOT make changes to the *original* Excel (or other) file that you import into Alteryx.

- Instead, Alteryx transforms the data you import into Designer according to the tools that you employ in your workflow.
  - o Reemphasizing the previous point, when you "import" data into Alteryx, you are not *moving* it there.
  - o Instead, you are effectively *copying* the source data for use in Alteryx while leaving the original data intact.

- Alteryx is frequently used to create an output file that reflects the changes you made to the original data.
  - o Consistent with the above explanations, this output file is *entirely separate* from the original file that you imported into Alteryx.

- As an example to illustrate these points:
  - o Let's assume that we extract 10,000 lines of sales data from the general ledger and save it to an Excel file.
  - o We use the use the "Input Data" tool to import the Excel file into Alteryx.
    - There will be more specifics on how to do this shortly.
  - o We then use Alteryx to organize, manipulate and modify the sales data.
  - o As a final step, we export the modified data from Alteryx and save it as a *separate* Excel file.
    - This is done using the "Output Data" tool, which will be covered later.
  - o At the end of the process, we have *two* Excel files.
    - The first is the original file with 10,000 lines of raw sales data.
    - The second is an updated file which, based on our Alteryx workflow, contains only the data that we want to see (e.g., the first quarter vs. the full year) and is presented in the format and layout that we want.

The SOX controls implications of unchanged original source data

- The Sarbanes-Oxley Act of 2002 ("SOX") places a significant emphasis on internal controls to improve the reliability and accuracy of financial reporting.

- A key aspect of good controls is ensuring that calculations are based on source data, or data or to information that's objective and verifiable.

- Examples of source data include:
    - Trial balance or general ledger detail.
    - Payroll data from HR.
    - Data from a previously filed tax return.
    - Data from a publicly available website.
        - Stock market data.
        - Foreign exchange rates.

- Almost all accounting, tax and financial professionals know to start their calculations with source data.

- However, a problem can arise when you start modifying source data to perform calculations.
    - Once you do this, it's no longer "pure" source data.
    - Further, it's more difficult to verify from a SOX point of view that the source data has not been materially altered in a way that could result in financial statement, tax return, or workpaper errors.

- An Excel-based solution would be to copy data before you start modifying it.
    - This would prove that your original source data is intact.
    - However, from a review perspective, one can only see that there are differences between the original and the modified file.
    - What a reviewer cannot often see is a clear trail that maps out exactly _how_ the data changed from its original to its modified form.

- Alteryx solves this problem as follows:
    - With Designer, you can easily confirm that source data is coming into the workflow (and this source data remains untouched and unchanged).
    - From there, you can evaluate how each tool in the workflow is impacts the data on the way to producing a modified file.

3.3   How to Use the "Input Data" Tool

The first steps to import data into Alteryx

- It's been necessary to cover a certain amount of background up to this point, but you're now equipped to dive into how to use Alteryx.

- To start practically any workflow, import data into Designer by following these steps.

  1) Drag an "Input Data" tool from the Tool Palette to the Canvas.
     - Since workflows run from left-to-right and the "Input Data" tool is the start of the workflow, I normally place this tool on the far left side of the Canvas.

  2) If it's not already selected, click on the "Input Data" tool that you placed on the Canvas.
     - This will bring up the tool's configuration window.
     - This same process/concept works for ALL tools – you click on any tool to bring its configuration window.

  3) In the configuration pictured below, click on the down arrow button at the far right of the field "Connect a File or Database."

Connect a File or Database

C:\Users\greent2\Desktop\TG Files\Alteryx\3.3 - Input Data\SalesJan2009.xlsx   ▼

Options

	Name	Value	
1	Record Limit		
2	File Format	Microsoft Excel (*.xlsx)	▼
3	Table or Query	`SalesJan2009$`	...
4	Search SubDirs	☐	
5	Output File Name as Field	No	▼
6	First Row Contains Data	☐	

Preview (first 100 records)   [Refresh]

	Transaction Date & Time	Product	Price	Payment Type	Name	City	
1	2009-01-02 06:17:00	Product1	1200	Mastercard	carolina	Basildon	
2	2009-01-02 04:53:00	Product1	1200	Visa	Betina	Parkville	
3	2009-01-02 13:08:00	Product1	1200	Mastercard	Federica e Andrea	Astoria	
4	2009-01-03 14:44:00	Product1	1200	Visa	Gouya	Echuca	
5	2009-01-04 12:56:00	Product2	3600	Visa	Gerd W	Cahaba Heig	
6	2009-01-04 13:19:00	Product1	1200	Visa	LAURENCE	Mickleton	
7	2009-01-04 20:11:00	Product1	1200	Mastercard	Fleur	Peoria	
8	2009-01-02 20:09:00	Product1	1200	Mastercard	adam	Martin	

  4) From there, click on
     - "Files."
     - "Select File."

o   After that, navigate to the data source (such as an Excel workbook) that you want to input import into the workflow.

o   Double-click the file after you locate it.

5) If an Input file doesn't connect, following are common reasons why.

o   The source file is currently open.

▪   You'll have to close the file for the "Input Data" tool to be able to read it.

o   The filepath of the source file has changed.

▪   If this is the case, you'll have to repeat the process above to point the "Input Data" tool to the file's new location.

6) In the case of an Excel workbook, click on "Select a sheet" to tell Alteryx which worksheet within the workbook you want to import.

o   This brings up an important point, which is that an "Input Data" tool can only import a _single_ sheet from an Excel workbook.

▪   Note, however, that you can use multiple "Import Data" tools if you need data from:

•   More than one Excel workbook.

•   More than one worksheet within the same Excel workbook.[7]

7) After you click "OK," the data will be imported into your workflow. You can preview it in the Configuration Window to make sure it's correct.

o   You will only be able to see the first 100 rows of data in the "Input Data" tool's preview pane.

o   However, this quick check is often enough to confirm that you imported the right data.

A shortcut – Drag source data files directly to the Canvas

•   The "long method" previously described is a safe, reliable way of importing data into an Alteryx workflow.

•   As a shortcut, you can drag an Excel (or other data) file to the Canvas, and it will _automatically_ create an "Input Data" tool with its filepath in the "Connect a File or Database" field filled in.

•   Once you know this shortcut and you've gotten used to it, it's unlikely you will use the "long method" again to import files except in rare cases.

---

[7] There is a tool called "Dynamic Input" (which is not covered in this material) that you may want to explore if you need to import data from numerous Excel workbooks into the same workflow.

3.4 Configuring the First Row of Your Dataset

Alteryx's default naming convention for the columns of imported data

- By default, the "Input Data" tool will interpret the first row of a dataset as "field names."
    - o "Field" is the Alteryx term that is often used for what Excel users call "columns."
    - o In this material, I will use the terms "field" and "column" synonymously.[8]

- The default setting described above fits the pattern of the dataset we imported into our workflow in the previous section (as pictured below), because the first row of that data contains column headers:
    - o Transaction Data & Time.
    - o Product.
    - o Price, etc.

	Transaction Date & Time	Product	Price	Payment Type	Name	City
1	2009-01-02 06:17:00	Product1	1200	Mastercard	carolina	Basildon
2	2009-01-02 04:53:00	Product1	1200	Visa	Betina	Parkville
3	2009-01-02 13:08:00	Product1	1200	Mastercard	Federica e Andrea	Astoria
4	2009-01-03 14:44:00	Product1	1200	Visa	Gouya	Echuca
5	2009-01-04 12:56:00	Product2	3600	Visa	Gerd W	Cahaba Heights

How to take control of which row is used to label the columns of imported data

- What if the first row of your dataset doesn't contain column (or field) headers? Instead, what if the very first row contains data?

- After importing such data, it would look something like the illustration that follows.

	2009-01-02 06:17:00	Product1	1200	Mastercard	carolina	Basildon
1	2009-01-02 04:53:00	Product1	1200	Visa	Betina	Parkville
2	2009-01-02 13:08:00	Product1	1200	Mastercard	Federica e Andrea	Astoria
3	2009-01-03 14:44:00	Product1	1200	Visa	Gouya	Echuca
4	2009-01-04 12:56:00	Product2	3600	Visa	Gerd W	Cahaba Heights
5	2009-01-04 13:19:00	Product1	1200	Visa	LAURENCE	Mickleton

---

[8] I'm doing this because most accounting, tax and finance professionals are heavy Excel users and are far more accustomed to the term "column." But when you refer to other Alteryx-related training and documentation, you will frequently encounter the term "field."

- Notice how Alteryx is using the first line from our imported sales data to name the various columns ("Product1," "1200," etc.).

- When you encounter a situation where the first row of your dataset contains data rather than column names (or headers), in the configuration for the "Input Data" tool you click the box, "First Row Contains Data."

6	First Row Contains Data	☑

- After doing so and clicking the "Refresh" button in the Configuration Window, the preview pane now shows the following:
  - The first row of your dataset now appears in "Line 1" as data.
  - Generic field names are provided for each column (F1, F2, F3, etc.).
    - Later we will cover how you can use the "Select" tool to rename columns from things such as "F1" to "Transaction Data & Time."

	F1	F2	F3	F4	F5	F6
1	2009-01-02 06:17:00	Product1	1200	Mastercard	carolina	Basildon
2	2009-01-02 04:53:00	Product1	1200	Visa	Betina	Parkville
3	2009-01-02 13:08:00	Product1	1200	Mastercard	Federica e Andrea	Astoria
4	2009-01-03 14:44:00	Product1	1200	Visa	Gouya	Echuca
5	2009-01-04 12:56:00	Product2	3600	Visa	Gerd W	Cahaba Heights

3.5   Other "Input Data" Configuration Settings

The "Refresh" button

- To elaborate further on the "Refresh" button just mentioned, let's assume the following:
  - We imported Excel sales data into our Alteryx workflow covering January through November.
  - Afterwards, December sales data becomes available, and we add this to our source Excel file as well.

- Now a question. Will your workflow automatically incorporate the December data that you added to the source Excel file?
  - The answer is no.

- You have to "push" updates made to source files into Alteryx in one of two ways.
  - The first is to click the "Refresh" button in the configuration of the "Input Data" tool that is connected to the data source you updated.
  - The second method is to click "Run" to process the entire workflow.

The "Record Limit" setting

- Previously, I noted that large datasets can slow down the processing time of a workflow.

- I also gave an example of a dataset with 100,000 lines of data, suggesting you could manually create a separate Excel file with just 1,000 lines of data to use while building out your workflow.

- As a shortcut, instead of creating a separate Excel file, you could configure the "Input Data" tool's "Record Limit" setting to 1,000 lines.

	Name	Value
1	Record Limit	1000

- This is much faster than the manual method described above, and it will significantly speed the processing time of your workflow.
    - This will allow you to use more effectively the "run as you go" workflow testing process that I previously recommended.
    - In this example, once your workflow is performing as intended, you can remove the value limit (i.e., delete the "1000") and it will process all 100,000 sales records when you click on "Run."

3.6   "Obvious" and "Obscure" Configuration Settings

- Since the "Input Data" tool is the first one that I'm covering in this material, I think it's a good time clarify my approach on covering "obvious" and "obscure" Alteryx tool configuration settings.

- In terms of "obvious," I didn't find it necessary to say that line two in the "Input Data" tool's configuration tells us that the file format imported into the workflow was an Excel file.

	Name	Value
1	Record Limit	
2	File Format	Microsoft Excel (*.xlsx)
3	Table or Query	`SalesJan2009$`

    - I think it's equally obvious that if a different file type is imported into Alteryx (e.g., a csv file) then that's what will populate in the "File Format" section.
    - In summary, when I believe something is obvious, I skip over it so that I can cover more material in less time.

- Likewise, if a configuration option is "obscure" from the vantage point of an accounting, tax, or finance professional, I also skip over it.
    - For example, by default, the "Input Data" tool's "Output File Name as Field" is set to "No."

5	Output File Name as Field	No

- However, if you select "Full Path," a column will be created at the far right of the output that shows the filepath and tab name of the source data.
- While it's conceivable this could have some application, I haven't found it to be an important part of effectively using Alteryx. As a result, I have skipped over providing a detailed explanation.

In summary, if I don't think a given Alteryx feature is relevant to most accounting, tax, and finance professionals, I don't spend time on it.

4 Organize the Top Section of Your Data

4.1   Learning Objectives

Upon the completion of this chapter, you will:

- Recognize the overarching importance of organizing your data prior to using it as the basis for calculations and how Alteryx fits into the process.
- Learn how to use the "Select Records" tool to manage the top section of your data.
- Learn how to use the "Dynamic Rename" tool to automatically name columns in data you import into Alteryx.

4.2   The Importance of Organizing Your Data for Calculations

The "calculation" is often straightforward

- One of the most compelling reasons for accounting, tax, and finance professionals to learn and use Alteryx is to organize data more efficiently prior to using it in Excel calculations.

- To illustrate, assume that you need to prepare a summary calculation analyzing R&D costs by division.
  - Conceptually, this is straightforward in that you need to:
    - Break out financial data by division.
    - Identify R&D employee compensation expense.
    - Determine other direct R&D costs (e.g., computer workstations used for R&D).
    - Calculate an overhead allocation attributable to R&D expenses.
  - Note that it only took me a few minutes to come up with all of that, and you could do the same.
    - The point: Many times, the "idea" behind a calculation isn't that hard, or doesn't take that long to develop, but the "execution" element of the same project can be like moving mountains.

"Data" is often the real problem

- So, what's the challenge? Why can't we use Excel to polish off our R&D analysis by lunch and be on to the next thing?

- The problem in this and in *many* other on-the-job examples lies in the quality of the data.
- In this specific example, assume the following:
  - The data dump from the GL by division is a messy text file filled with delimiters.
  - There are numerous breaks in the body of the data.
  - The same heading appears at the top of each page.
  - Data for eight of the company's divisions is housed in one ERP system, but the other two are stored in another ERP system and the format is completely different.
  - R&D expenses are booked in separate accounts in the GL, and some of the data is mixed in with other types of expenses.

- Does this sound familiar? In our line of work, both you and I could go on and on listing potential problems with data but, whatever they are, we arrive at the same place:
  - If you're using Excel as your *only* tool to tackle data-related challenges, you've got a massive amount of manual, tedious, and time-consuming effort in front of you.

How Alteryx fits in

- There is a better way, there is a faster way, and there is even a more *enjoyable* way to tackle data-related challenges, and it involves the use of Alteryx.

- Specifically for our R&D example, I would recommend that we FIRST use Alteryx to prepare and organize our data.

- After that, THEN I would recommend that we export our clean, uniform, and perfectly formatted data to Excel to perform our R&D analysis.

- I don't mean to be repetitive, but it's vitally important that you understand this key point: I am NOT advocating that you abandon Excel in favor of Alteryx.
  - Excel is outrageously powerful, flexible, and extremely well-suited to perform customized computations.
  - I would *never* try to convince an accounting, tax, or finance professional to abandon Excel for this and many other reasons![9]

- What I am saying is that Alteryx is an exceptionally powerful COMPLIMENT to Excel, able to perform many data-related tasks with far greater speed and accuracy than would ever be possible using Excel alone, even with the sophisticated use of formulas and functions.

---

[9] For me personally, I would have no problem giving up Excel…after you pry it from my cold, dead hands. ☺

- With this in mind, the purpose of the rest of this chapter (and the next several that follow) is to teach you Alteryx tools and techniques that will enable you to transform large, complex, and messy datasets into formats that are clean, organized, and ready for your use in Excel calculations.

4.3 Manage Rows with the "Select Records" Tool

Data rarely comes into a workflow exactly the way you want

- A common problem when importing data into Alteryx is there are unnecessary and/or empty rows at the top of the dataset.

- As an example, consider a sales report that looks like this in Excel.

Sales Report for Company X
Period: Q1 2021

Transaction_date	Product	Price	Payment_Type	Name
1/2/2009 6:17	Product1	1,200	Mastercard	carolina
1/2/2009 4:53	Product1	1,200	Visa	Betina
1/2/2009 13:08	Product1	1,200	Mastercard	Federica e Andrea
1/3/2009 14:44	Product1	1,200	Visa	Gouya

- After you use the "Input Data" tool to import this data into your Alteryx workflow, you will see this at the top of the preview pane (which is not at all what you want!).

	Sales Report for Company X	F2	F3	F4	F5
1	Period: Q1 2020	[Null]	[Null]	[Null]	[Null]
2	[Null]	[Null]	[Null]	[Null]	[Null]
3	[Null]	[Null]	[Null]	[Null]	[Null]
4	Transaction_date	Product	Price	Payment_Type	Name
5	2009-01-02 06:17:00	Product1	1200	Mastercard	carolina
6	2009-01-02 04:53:00	Product1	1200	Visa	Betina
7	2009-01-02 13:08:00	Product1	1200	Mastercard	Federica e Andrea
8	2009-01-03 14:44:00	Product1	1200	Visa	Gouya

Use the "Select Records" tool to remove unnecessary rows of data

- In this example, how do we remove:
    - The title of the sales report ("Sales Report for Company X") from the "fields row" and

- How do we remove the unneeded and empty rows (containing "null" or empty values) in lines1-3?

- To start the process, we'll use the "Select Records" tool. Drag it from the Tool Palette to the Canvas and place it next to the "Input Data" tool.

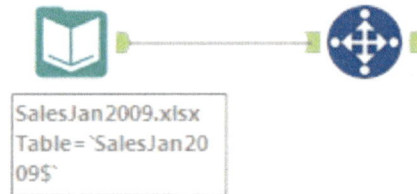

SalesJan2009.xlsx
Table=`SalesJan20
09$`

  - Note: You need to place "Select Records" tool close enough to "Input Data" tool that the two connect with a black line (this means the tools can now "talk to each other").
  - This same approach applies to all tools – you need to make sure they are connected to each other (as signified by a black line between them) or there will be a break in your workflow.

- After the "Select Records" is on the Canvas, click on it to bring up its configuration (see the illustration below).

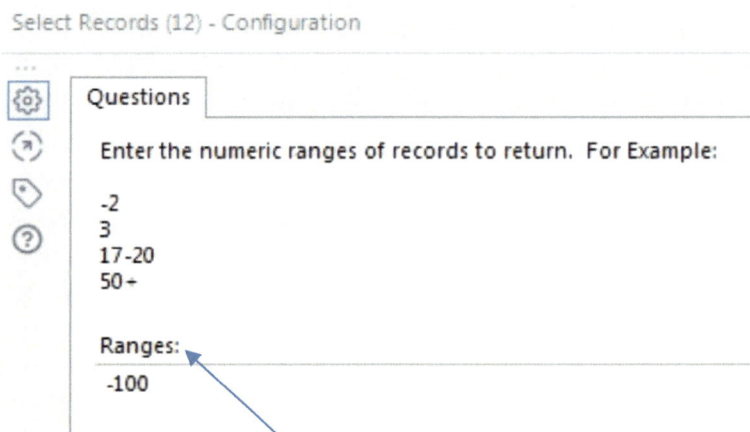

Select Records (12) - Configuration

Questions

Enter the numeric ranges of records to return. For Example:

-2
3
17-20
50+

Ranges:

-100

- To clarify what you're seeing, here is what would appear in the Results Window after you ran the workflow if you configured the "Ranges" section of the "Select Records" tool with the following:
  - -2   You would see only the first two rows of the incoming data.
  - 3   Out of the entire incoming dataset, only row 3 would be displayed.
  - 17-20   Rows 17-20 would display, but nothing else.
  - 50+   This would display the imported data starting from row 50.
  - -100   Only the first 100 lines of the incoming data would display.

Configuring the "Select Records" tool

- In our example, none of the configuration options above is exactly what we're looking for, but the "50+" option is the closest.

- o In other words, rather than skipping the first 50 lines of the data imported into our workflow from the "Input Data" tool, we want our cleaned up dataset to start with the row containing the names "Transaction_date," Product," "Price," etc.

- Accomplishing this is trickier than it first appears. Here is one of the reasons why.
  - o First, note that the column descriptions ("Transaction_date," etc.) in the original *Excel* source data appear on row 5.

	Sales Report for Company X	Product	Price	Payment_Type	Name
1	**Sales Report for Company X**				
2	**Period: Q1 2021**				
3					
4					
5	Transaction_date	Product	Price	Payment_Type	Name
6	1/2/2009 6:17	Product1	1,200	Mastercard	carolina
7	1/2/2009 4:53	Product1	1,200	Visa	Betina
8	1/2/2009 13:08	Product1	1,200	Mastercard	Federica e Andrea

- However, if you look in Alteryx's "Input Data's" preview pane, you will see that the column descriptions begin in row 4.

	Sales Report for Company X	F2	F3	F4	F5
1	Period: Q1 2021	[Null]	[Null]	[Null]	[Null]
2	[Null]	[Null]	[Null]	[Null]	[Null]
3	[Null]	[Null]	[Null]	[Null]	[Null]
4	Transaction_date	Product	Price	Payment_Type	Name
5	2009-01-02 06:17:00	Product1	1200	Mastercard	carolina
6	2009-01-02 04:53:00	Product1	1200	Visa	Betina
7	2009-01-02 13:08:00	Product1	1200	Mastercard	Federica e Andrea

- So, what determines how "Select Records" should be configured, the data's position in the original source file (Excel) or its position in the "Input Data" tool?
  - o The answer is that Designer looks to the data's position in the "Input Data" tool.
  - o With that in mind, if we configure the "Select Records" configuration with "4+," the output displayed in the Results Window (after running the workflow) is as follows.

	Sales Report for Company X	F2	F3	F4	F5
1	Transaction_date	Product	Price	Payment_Type	Name
2	2009-01-02 06:17:00	Product1	1200	Mastercard	carolina
3	2009-01-02 04:53:00	Product1	1200	Visa	Betina
4	2009-01-02 13:08:00	Product1	1200	Mastercard	Federica e Andrea

- This is definitely an improvement; we're gotten rid of some extraneous rows and the "Transaction_date" and other column descriptions now appear in line 1 of our data.
  - However, there is still a problem.
  - Being in the row labeled "1" means Alteryx is reading that information as DATA and NOT as column headers.
    - To clarify, the column headers in the illustration above are currently "Sales Report for Company X," "F2," "F3," etc.

The "Input Data" tool determines how the first row of data is treated

- How do we fix this? How do we get Alteryx to use the row we want to populate the column ("field") names?

- By default, the "Input Data" tool will read the first row of imported data as column (or "field") headers UNLESS the "First Row Contains Data" box within the tool's configuration is checked.

6 First Row Contains Data	✓

- After checking this box and clicking "Refresh" in the "Input Data" tool, the first row of imported data now looks like this.

	F1	F2	F3	F4	F5	F6
1	Sales Report for Company X	[Null]	[Null]	[Null]	[Null]	[Null]
2	Period: Q1 2021	[Null]	[Null]	[Null]	[Null]	[Null]
3	[Null]	[Null]	[Null]	[Null]	[Null]	[Null]
4	[Null]	[Null]	[Null]	[Null]	[Null]	[Null]
5	Transaction_date	Product	Price	Payment_Type	Name	City
6	2009-01-02 06:17:00	Product1	1200	Mastercard	carolina	Basildon

- Notice that checking the "First Row Contains Data" box caused the following to happen:
  - Since Alteryx is now reading ALL imported information from the Excel file as data, the columns have been assigned generic names (F1, F2, etc.).
    - And, for our example, the first row of the Excel file (containing the title "Sales Report for Company X") is now being treated in Alteryx as a data field.
    - In addition, the row containing the column names we want has shifted down from line 4 to line 5 in the illustration above.

Fine tuning the "Select Records" configuration and determining the next steps

- With the data now being read into the workflow as described above, this is what we see in the "Results Window" if we update the configuration of the "Select Records" tool from "4+" to "5+."
  - o We've done this because we want Alteryx to start importing data starting at line 5 (see the previous illustration).

	F1	F2	F3	F4	F5
1	Transaction_date	Product	Price	Payment_Type	Name
2	2009-01-02 06:17:00	Product1	1200	Mastercard	carolina
3	2009-01-02 04:53:00	Product1	1200	Visa	Betina

- To summarize where we are:
  - o We've used the "Select Records" tool to remove the unneeded rows from the top of the dataset.
  - o The row containing our column descriptions is now the first line of data ("Transaction_date," etc.).
  - o HOWEVER, we want the descriptions in line 1 above to replace the generic column descriptions F1, F2, etc.
  - o To do this, we will need to add another tool to the workflow called "Dynamic Rename," which is covered in the next section.

4.4 Use the "Dynamic Rename" Tool to Make the First Row of Data Your Column Names

Finding the "Dynamic Rename" tool

- To use the "Dynamic Rename" tool, you first need to FIND it, which is not obvious.
  - o It's not in the "Favorites" section of the Tool Palette.

- "Dynamic Rename" is located in the "Developer" section of the Tool Palette.
  - o "But wait," you might say, "I don't see a 'Developer' section?"
  - o This is because it doesn't fit on most screens.
  - o To get there, you need to click the arrow at the far right of the Tool Palette.
    - ▪ On my monitor, it's located beside the purple "Calgary" section.

- After clicking on the right arrow (perhaps multiple times), you will finally see the "Developer" section.

- After clicking on the "Developer" section, you will see the "Dynamic Rename" tool.

Add the "Dynamic Rename" tool (or ANY tool) to your "Favorites"

- After going through all the effort to find the "Dynamic Rename" tool, you may want to add it to your "Favorites" section in the Tool Palette.

- To do so, right-click on the tool in the Tool Palette section (not on the Canvas) and select "Add to Favorites."

- After doing so, click on the "Favorites" section on the far left side of the Tool Palette.

- There you will see the "Dynamic Rename" tool has been added, and it has a yellow star beside it.

- If you wish to reposition the tool in the Favorites section:
  - Move your cursor over it.
  - Your "arrow" curser will transfer into a "cross arrows" cursor.
    - You may need to click on the tool if this doesn't automatically happen.
  - After the "cross arrows" appears, hold down the mouse button and reposition the tool to where you would like it to be going forward.
  - The tool will maintain its position unless you move it again or you uncheck the yellow box to designate that it's no longer a Favorite.

- The process above works for ANY tool in the Tool Palette.

Configuring "Dynamic Rename" to convert the first row of data to column names

- To automatically convert the first row of data (or "line 1") to column names, follow these steps:
  - Drag the "Dynamic Rename" tool to the Canvas and place it to the right of "Select Records."
    - Note that the "Select Records" tool should automatically connect to the left input anchor (marked "L") of the "Dynamic Rename" tool.
    - After doing this, our workflow should look like the illustration.

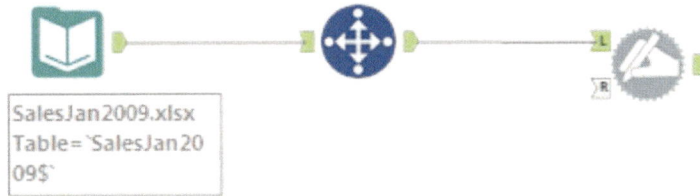

SalesJan2009.xlsx
Table= `SalesJan20
09$`

- From here, we need to configure the "Dynamic Rename" tool. To do so, click on it.

- In the "Rename Mode" drop-down, select "Take Field Names from First Row of Data" (see the illustration below).
   - After doing this, you will see checkmarks appear in the boxes F1, F2, F3, etc.
   - These are the CURRENT names of the existing fields (or columns) in our data.
   - The checkmarks mean that each of these fields will be replaced by the information that's in the first row of the data which, in our case, are the column names that we want ("Transaction_date," etc.).

Rename Mode: | Take Field Names from First Row of Data | ▼

☑ F1	▲	All
☑ F2	☰	
☑ F3		Clear
☑ F4		
☑ F5		
☑ F6	▼	

- After clicking "Run" to process the workflow, we will see the following in the Results Window.

	Transaction_date	Product	Price	Payment_Type	Name
1	2009-01-02 06:17:00	Product1	1200	Mastercard	carolina
2	2009-01-02 04:53:00	Product1	1200	Visa	Betina
3	2009-01-02 13:08:00	Product1	1200	Mastercard	Federica e Andrea
4	2009-01-03 14:44:00	Product1	1200	Visa	Gouya

- Congratulations! You have succeeded in the first step of taking control of your data, which was automating the process of:
   - Removing unwanted rows at the beginning of the dataset and
   - Using information that already existed in the data to name the columns.

5 Exporting Data from Alteryx Using the "Output Data" Tool

5.1 Learning Objectives

Upon the completion of this chapter, you will:

- Learn how to use and configure the "Output Data" tool to export your data from Alteryx in a format that you can use for Excel calculations.
- Know the steps to take to resolve "Output Data" errors.
- Be able to name other software programs that can read exported data from Alteryx.
- Complete your very first Alteryx workflow.

5.2 How to Export Data to a New File Using the "Output Data" Tool

The purpose of the "Output Data" tool

- Based on the sales data example we've been working on, let's assume for a moment that we're now satisfied with the updated format and layout of the data.

- That begs the question, how do we export the cleaned up data from Alteryx so that we can use it in Excel calculations?

- The answer is that you will use the "Output Data" tool to export your data.

How to use and configure the "Output Data" tool

- Drag the "Output Data" tool from the "Favorites" section of the Tool Palette to the Canvas, placing it next to "Dynamic Rename" (as illustrated below).

- After doing so, configure the "Output Data" tool by clicking on it.

- From there, click on the down arrow in the section "Write to File or Database" to select where you want to save your cleaned up and organized data.

Write to File or Database

C:\Users\greent2\Desktop\TG Files\Alteryx\5.2 - Output Data\Clean Sales Data.xlsx|||Sheet1   ▼

Setting the filepath to save your data

- For the present example, we're going to name our new file "Clean Sales Data" and save it to a folder called "5.2 – Output Data."
  - This is shown in the illustration above.

- This is done as follows:
  - As noted above, the first step is to click on the down arrow in the section "Write to File or Database."
  - Click "Files."
  - Click "Select File."
  - Navigate to the folder "5.2 – Output Data."

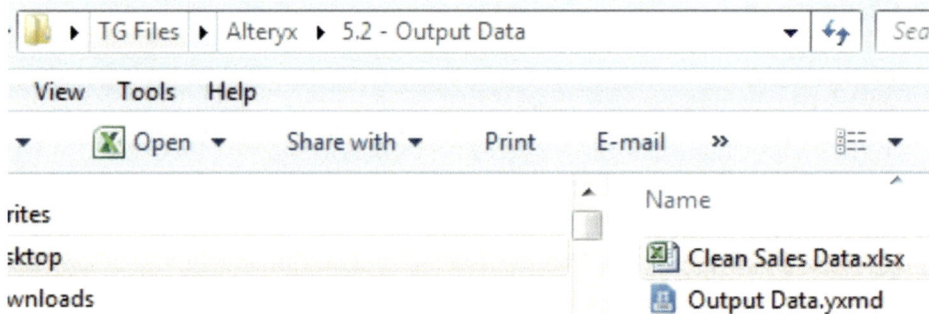

▸ TG Files ▸ Alteryx ▸ 5.2 - Output Data	▼ ↳	Sea

View Tools Help

▼   [X] Open ▼   Share with ▼   Print   E-mail   »   ▤ ▼

rites

sktop   Name

wnloads   [X] Clean Sales Data.xlsx

                                    Output Data.yxmd

  - In the "Filename" field type "Clean Sales Data."
  - Click "Save" to save the file in the default Excel format.
  - Your data will now be saved to a single sheet in a new Excel workbook.
    - At this point, you can accept the default of "Sheet1" as the name of the worksheet.
    - You could also choose another name for the worksheet such as "Sales Summary."
  - After this, click "OK."

- So, did a new Excel file save after you clicked "OK" in the last step?
  - The answer is no.
  - By taking the steps above, you have only told Alteryx _where_ to save your exported file (or your "output").

- To produce the new Excel file and export it to the location you designated above, you need to *run the workflow*.

Exporting file types other than Excel

- In the example above, we saved our updated file to an Excel format. However, it's helpful to know that there are *many* other options depending on your needs.

- Prior to clicking "Save" to designate the file location of your exported data, take a look at the options in the "Save as type" field (click the down arrow).

File name:	Clean Sales Data.xlsx	▼
Save as type:	Microsoft Excel (*.xlsx)	▼

- While Excel is the default file type for exporting your data (as shown above), you can export data that's compatible with other software programs such as:
  - Comma Separated Value (.csv)
  - Hyper Text Markup Language (.htm)
  - Microsoft Access
  - SAS
  - Tableau
  - Plus several others.

5.3   More on Configuring the "Output Data" Tool

Encountering errors when you attempt to export data

- As noted above, after you run your workflow, you'll now have a new Excel file called "Clean Sales" data in the folder "5.2 – Output Data."

- What happens if you run the workflow again right away?
  - The answer is you'll get an error that looks like this.

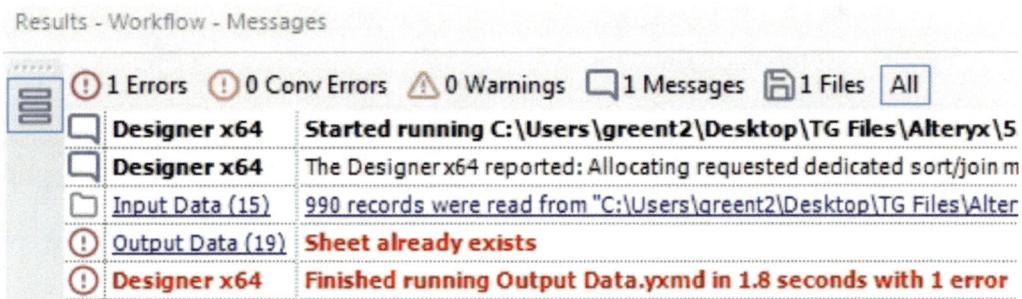

Results - Workflow - Messages

	⊙ 1 Errors ⊙ 0 Conv Errors ⚠ 0 Warnings ⬜ 1 Messages ⊟ 1 Files All	
	Designer x64	Started running C:\Users\greent2\Desktop\TG Files\Alteryx\5
	Designer x64	The Designer x64 reported: Allocating requested dedicated sort/join m
	Input Data (15)	990 records were read from "C:\Users\greent2\Desktop\TG Files\Alter
	Output Data (19)	Sheet already exists
	Designer x64	Finished running Output Data.yxmd in 1.8 seconds with 1 error

- Looking at this more closely (your first workflow error!), you see in the message above, "Sheet already exists."
  - In addition, if you look at your workflow you will see a red exclamation point on the "Output Data" tool.
  - This is telling you that this particular tool is causing the error.

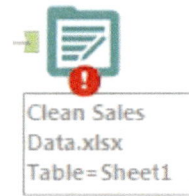

Clean Sales
Data.xlsx
Table=Sheet1

- What happened? Why do you get an error message when you try to save your exported file again?

Alternatives for "Output Options" and what they mean

- The answer to the questions above lies in how the "Output Options" setting is configured.
  - By default, this is set to "Create New Sheet."

Options	
Name	Value
1 Max Records Per File	
2 File Format	Microsoft Excel (*.xlsx)
3 Output Options	Create New Sheet
4 Append Field Map	By Field Name
5 Skip Field Names	

  - More specifically, this means a new Excel file will be created after you run the workflow.
  - However, Alteryx cannot execute this action – that of creating a *new* file – if an Excel file already exists with the same name and file location.

- To resolve the error, you will need to do one of the following.
  - Change the name of your output file.
    - For example, instead of "Clean Sales Data," you could name the new file "Clean Sales Data – 2."
  - Another option is to change the "Output Options" to "Overwrite File (Remove)."

Options	
Name	Value
1 Max Records Per File	
2 File Format	Microsoft Excel (*.xlsx)
3 Output Options	Overwrite File (Remove)

    - In our example, when the workflow is re-run it will delete and save over the previous version of "Clean Sales Data."
    - Any changes in the old version of "Clean Sales Data" will be lost.

- Other "Output Options" are as follows:
  - "Overwrite Sheet (Drop)"

- This is like "Overwrite File (Remove)" in that it will delete the existing sheet in the "Clean Sales Data" file and save the updated one.
    - I find this option to be redundant, opting for "Overwrite File (Remove)" instead.
  o "Append to Existing Sheet"
    - This option doesn't delete the data in the last version. Instead, it adds the new and updated data starting where the old version left off.
        - I have never found a practical use for this option.

- In summary:
  o By default, when using "Output Data," you cannot save over the prior version.
  o Instead, you either need to:
    - Change the filename or location if your output or
    - Select the "Overwrite File (Remove)" output option.

Comments on other "Output Data" configuration options

- Are there other configuration options for the "Output Data" tool? Absolutely. At this point, am I going to cover any more of them? Absolutely not.

- As I've previously stated, the purpose of this material is focus on Alteryx-related features necessary to be effective as accounting, tax, and finance professionals.

- In my estimation, you know everything you need to about the "Output Data" tool for now, and I believe your time will be better spent on new material.
  o I will follow this same pattern as we cover other Alteryx features and tools.

5.4 The "Output Data" Tool Represents the Completion of a Workflow

Defining the completion of a workflow

- At this point you've hit a major milestone in your growing knowledge of Alteryx – *you've completed your first workflow!*

- Exactly what does that mean? I define a complete workflow process as follows:

  1) Import
     - You import a data file into Alteryx (using an "Input Data" tool).
  2) Analyze and Organize
     - You organize, modify, format, clean, manipulate and analyze that data according to your needs (using a variety of Alteryx tools).
  3) Export

- After you have accomplished everything you need to with your data and it's in the format that you want, you export it to an external file (using an "Output Data" tools).

Now you're on the verge of conquering the world of data!

- Most all workflows – whether they contain 3 tools or 300 – follow the simple pattern that I've described above.
  - This concept has both powerful and exciting implications.

- It means that now you truly know how to create Alteryx workflows. From this point you will now:
  - *Broaden your knowledge* of the Alteryx tools available to use,
  - *Delve more deeply* into how to use these tools effectively and
  - *Successfully address and resolve* progressively more varied and sophisticated *data-related challenges*.

In addition, you can have a deeper sense of professional fulfillment along the way, because it's far more interesting and engaging to resolve data-related challenges by applying Alteryx's software tools coupled with your own thinking and logic verses dealing with the same issues using the brute force of manual (and tedious) manipulation of Excel spreadsheets!

6 A Deeper Dive into Alteryx Tool and Workflow Features

6.1 Learning Objectives

Upon the completion of this chapter, you will:

- Have a deeper and more commanding knowledge of the options and features available on Alteryx's main screen as you work with your data.
- Be able to use input and output anchors to follow your data as it progresses through your workflow.
- Learn the significance of errors, how to know what's causing them, as well as how to troubleshoot what's causing them.
- Know how to organize and sort data in the Results Window to gain greater insight into your output.
- Recognize the need to invest the thought, time, and effort into keeping your workflows simple, as well as strategies for how to do so.

6.2 The Vital Need to Prepare for Launch

- With the knowledge you can now create workflows, it may be tempting to launch headlong into learning new tools, throwing them on the Canvas in spades in the creation of ever more sophisticated workflows.

- However, before too hastily going into overdrive, it's helpful to remember some sage advice from Han Solo to Luke Skywalker:
    o "Traveling through hyperspace ain't like dusting crops, boy! Without precise calculations we could fly right through a star or bounce too close to a supernova and that'd end your trip real quick, wouldn't it?"[10]

- Here's the point. In the sales example we've been working through so far, we've only removed a few rows from the top of a dataset that's roughly 1,000 lines.
    o How badly could we have messed that up?
    o Even if our workflow wasn't configured correctly, we could easily do some manual cleanup in Excel on the _back end_ to tidy things up.
    o Alternatively, we could have done some manual cleanup of data on the _front end_ to reduce our need to use Alteryx tools, thus simplifying our workflow.

---

[10] From Start Wars Episode IV: "A New Hope."

- In other words, how hard would it have been in our sales example to just delete a few rows from the top of the dataset prior to importing it into Alteryx?

- It can be tempting to think along those lines, especially if you're an experienced Excel user. But that mentality completely misses the mark on a number of different levels.
    - Automation – We're not using Alteryx to add more manual steps to our work; we're using Alteryx to *automate* data-related organization and analysis.
    - Sure, a little manual manipulation wouldn't take much time in our sales dataset with just 1,000 lines. But what if we're talking about 10,000, 100,000, or even 1 million lines of data?
        - When you're dealing with datasets of that size, manual manipulation simply doesn't cut it.
        - To have to approach problems that way is the equivalent of being in a white-collar prison where you would hit numbers with your Excel sledgehammer for hours on end, day in and day out.[11]
        - In summary, my purpose for showing you how to use Alteryx with small, digestible examples is to equip you to deal with *much larger* ones.
    - Frequency – Volume isn't the only issue that takes time; frequency can be just as important.
        - In our sales example we're just producing a single data file, but what if that file had to be produced:
            - Monthly, weekly, daily, or even hourly?
            - Would you still be up for a manual manipulation approach?
        - Alternatively, what if the same sales report – a report for a single store – had to be produced for all 887 stores in your company?
            - Do you want to manually scrub your sales data 887 times before you're ready to analyze it?

- The point I'm trying to drive home is that striving to use Alteryx knowledgably and according to its maximum capabilities (vs. "kinda-sorta" knowing it) will enable you to fully capture the benefits of its power, speed, and scale.
    - Said another way, if you learn how to use Alteryx the right way, avoiding manual shortcuts, you'll develop the ability to organize and analyze vast amounts of data quickly and skillfully.

- With these things in mind, before moving on to learning new tools, we're going to take a closer look at some key features of Alteryx Designer.

---

[11] If you manually adjusted one line of data a second in a spreadsheet with 1,000,000 lines, it would take you 278 hours – or almost seven work weeks – to finish the task. Oh, and that's working straight through without eating or sleeping.

6.3   Revisiting the Alteryx Screen's Layout

By now, you have a basic level of familiarity with the various areas of the Designer workspace, but let's explore some of these sections in more detail.

Explore the Tool Palette

- So far, you're only familiar with the tools that I've presented to you.

- Of course, I will be showing you more as we progress through this material. But even by the end, we won't come close to covering all the Alteryx tools that are available.

- Also, while we're all accounting, tax and finance professionals who share many commonalities in our work, we still have a significant amount of variability in our areas of specialization, our industries, and our companies.

- Because of this, I believe it's worth taking the time to go beyond the "Favorites" and to explore different Tool Palette categories such as:
  - "In/Out"
  - "Preparation"
  - "Join," etc.

- By doing this, you will likely get ideas that will help you to tailor your learning of Alteryx in a way that makes you more effective in your specific roles and responsibilities.

- Note that the names of many Alteryx tools are intuitive, but many are not.
  - Either way, you can learn more about a tool by right-clicking on it while it's still in the Tool Palette (and not on the Canvas).
  - And remember, from there you can:
    - Click "Help" to read a description of the tool, what it does, and how it works.
    - Click "Open Example" to see in a "hands-on" way of how the tool functions in an actual workflow.

Tabs for multiple workflows

- Similar to the way Internet browser tabs work, you can have more than one workflow open at a time.

- Click on the tabs (pictured below) to alternate back and forth between workflows.

Explore the dropdown menus

- Use the "File" section to open, save, and print workflows.
  - "File – Open Recent" is also handy for quickly opening a workflow you were in recently.

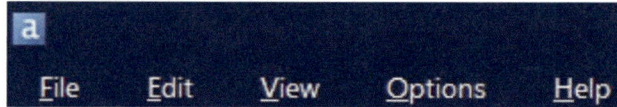

- The "Edit" section contains commands such as cut, copy and paste but, in practice, much of that is done by clicking and right-clicking, as well as by using "Control" shortcuts.
  - Control-X – Cut
  - Control-C – Copy
  - Control-V – Paste
  - Control-Z – Undo

- The "View" section allows you to control what sections you see on the screen.
  - For example, you could hide the Results Window if you wanted more screen space devoted to your actual workflow.
  - While it's certainly nice to have this option, I rarely use in practice. I find it useful to have all the areas of the Alteryx screen in view.

- You can adjust the size of areas on the Alteryx screen to suit your needs.
  - In the example below, both the Configuration Widow and the Results Window are presently taking up a massive amount of screen space, to the point that the workflow barely fits on the screen.

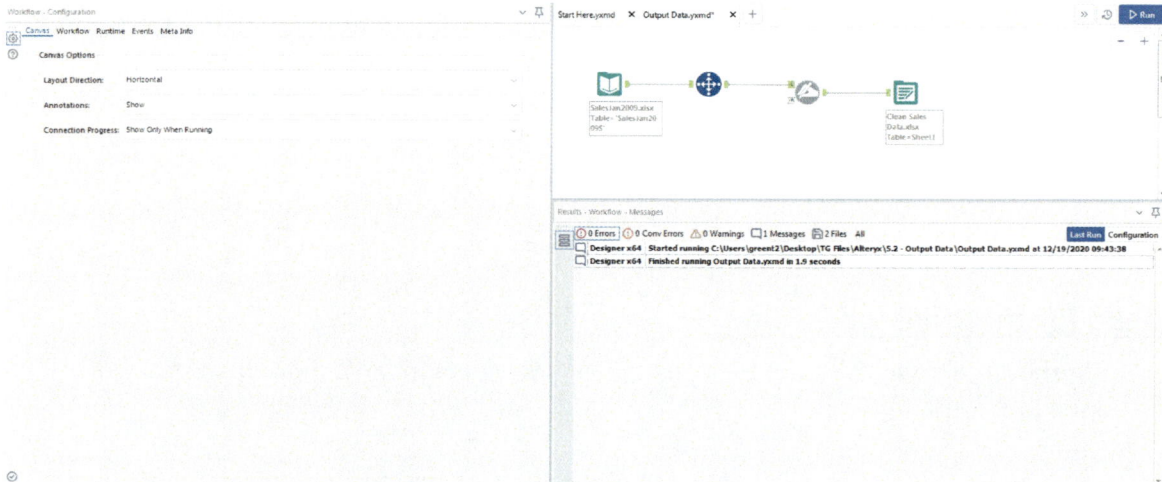

- By positioning your cursor on the vertical and horizontal lines between the different sections of Designer, you can adjust their size.

- By doing so, you can create more space to view your workflow (as shown below).

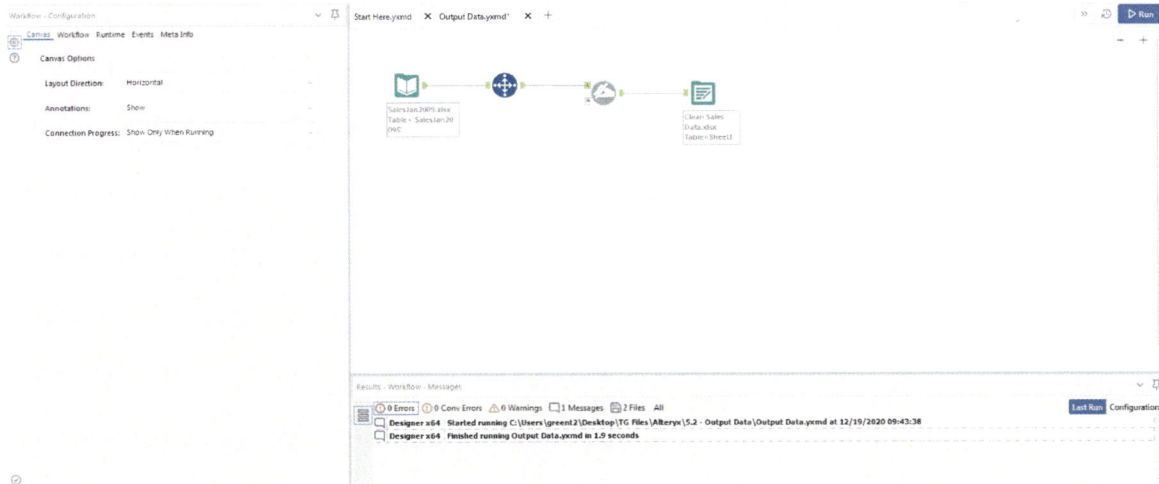

Moving around the Canvas and adjusting the size of the tools

- As your workflows grow in size and sophistication, they may not fit on fit on the screen (like they do in our simple example above).

- When a workflow extends past the visible screen, navigation bars appear to the right and at the bottom of the Canvas so you can scroll to the area where you need to work.
    - After clicking anywhere on the Canvas, you can also use the wheel on your mouse to scroll up and down within a workflow.

- You can also adjust the size of the tools in your workflow by clicking the "+" and "-" buttons below "Run" button. ———— the

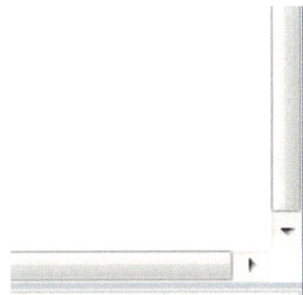

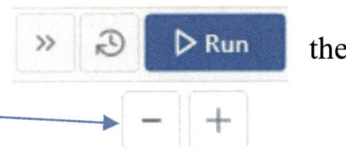

6.4 Following Data through Your Workflow as it Passes Through Tools

Use input and output anchors of tools to follow your data

- Up to this point, it's possible to have had the mistaken impression that after you click "Run" to process your workflow, you can only see in the Results Window what your data looks like in its *final* form.

- That's not at all the case. In fact, you see what's how Alteryx tools are impacting your data as it passes through *each step* of the workflow.

- Referring to the workflow we created before, notice that the "Input Data" tool has a small yellowish-green arrow on its right side.

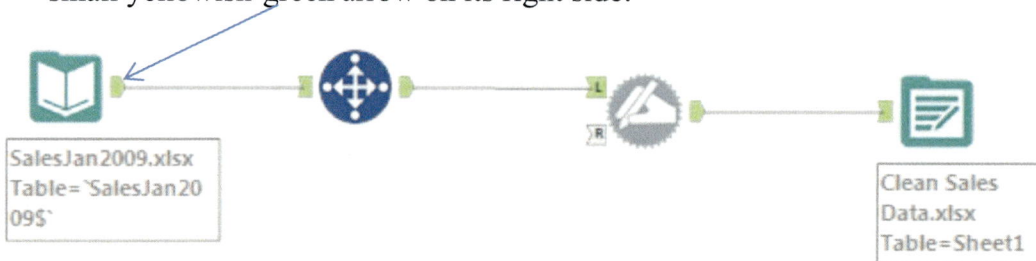

SalesJan2009.xlsx
Table=`SalesJan20
09$`

Clean Sales
Data.xlsx
Table=Sheet1

- These are referred to as "anchors."
  - Anchors that appear on the left side of tools are called "input anchors."
  - Anchors that appear on the right side of tools are known as "output anchors."
  - Some tools have more than one input and/or output anchor.
    - For example, as shown above, the "Dynamic Rename" tool has two input anchors, labeled left ("L") and right ("R").

- If you click on a tool's input anchor, you can see how data looks as it flows into it in the Results Window.
  - You must run the workflow for this to be the case.

- If you click on a tool's output anchor then *you can determine what the tool did to the data*, which is the form it will take as it makes its way to the next tool in the workflow.

An example of how to follow your data through a workflow

- Let's continue with our example in the illustration above to see how this works.

- As a first step, we'll run the workflow, because that will push our data through all of the tools.

- Now, starting with the "Input Data" tool at the beginning of the workflow, notice that there is no input anchor.
  - This is because the "Input Data" tool is importing data from outside of Alteryx, i.e., the data is not coming from another tool.
  - If you click on the tool's output anchor then, in the Results Window, you can see what the data looks like as it first comes into the workflow (see the illustration that follows).
    - Note: You can see some of this data in the "Input Data" tool's preview box in the Configuration Window, but you get a much clearer view of it in the Results Window (again, pictured below).

F1	F2	F3	F4	F5
1 Sales Report for Company X	[Null]	[Null]	[Null]	[Null]
2 Period: Q1 2021	[Null]	[Null]	[Null]	[Null]
3 [Null]	[Null]	[Null]	[Null]	[Null]
4 [Null]	[Null]	[Null]	[Null]	[Null]
5 Transaction_date	Product	Price	Payment_Type	Name
6 2009-01-02 06:17:00	Product1	1200	Mastercard	carolina
7 2009-01-02 04:53:00	Product1	1200	Visa	Betina

- When you click on the input anchor of the "Select Records" tool then the data will look EXACTLY the same as it does when you click on the output anchor of the "Input Data" tool.

- When you click on the output anchor of the "Select Records" tool, you will see that it's removed all the extra (pr "null") rows from the top of the dataset.

F1	F2	F3	F4	F5
1 Transaction_date	Product	Price	Payment_Type	Name
2 2009-01-02 06:17:00	Product1	1200	Mastercard	carolina
3 2009-01-02 04:53:00	Product1	1200	Visa	Betina

- Following the pattern described previously, when you click the left ("L") input anchor the "Dynamic Rename" tool, the data looks exactly the same as it did going OUT of the "Select Records" tool.
    - o The "Dynamic Rename" tool has two input anchors.
    - o When using it to renaming columns, Alteryx practically forces you to connect to the left ("L") input anchor.
    - o However, for other tools that will be introduced later (such as the "Join" tool), you need to be more deliberate in choosing which input anchor of a given tool to connect to.

- After clicking on the output anchor of "Dynamic Rename," you can confirm that the tool successfully converted the first line of data to field (or column) names.

Transaction_date	Product	Price	Payment_Type	Name
1 2009-01-02 06:17:00	Product1	1200	Mastercard	carolina
2 2009-01-02 04:53:00	Product1	1200	Visa	Betina
3 2009-01-02 13:08:00	Product1	1200	Mastercard	Federica e Andrea

- Finally, when you click on the input anchor of the "Output Data" tool, you will see the data in the same condition that it was in when it left the "Dynamic Rename" tool.
    - o Also note that the "Output Data" tool doesn't have an output anchor.
    - o This is because "Output Data" doesn't pass data on to another tool but exports it outside of the Alteryx environment (to an Excel file, for example).

Summary

- The point of this section is that it doesn't have to be a mystery of what's happening to your data as it's passing through your workflow!
  - As illustrated above, you can review what's happening to your data at every step of the way by clicking on the input and out anchors of tools and evaluating the output in the Results Window.

- Knowing this allows you to do as I previously recommended, which is to run your workflow at each stage that you're building it.
  - This will enable you to test your workflow as you go, ensuring that your data is being handled and transformed the way you intended.

- Once you feel your workflow is processing correctly then, as a final check, you can open the output file (e.g., the Excel file you exported) to do a more complete review prior to using the data in your calculations.

6.5   The Results Window

- After you run your workflow, there's a lot of useful information in the Results which we will now review together.

Gaining insight into errors

- An important function of the Results Window is to give you more insight into what's causing errors in your workflow.
  - We've previously compared a workflow to water flowing through a canal.
  - Think of an error as something that's creating a blockage in the canal, preventing the water (or data) from reaching its destination (an "Output Data" tool) and accomplishing what you intended along the way.

- We previously encountered an error when we tried to use the "Output Data" tool to export to a file location where that file already existed.

- Following is another example of an error that has to do with the "Select Records" tool (see the red exclamation point in the illustration that follows).

[This space was intentionally left blank].

SalesJan2009.xlsx
Table=`SalesJan20
09$`

Clean Sales
Data.xlsx
Table=Sheet1

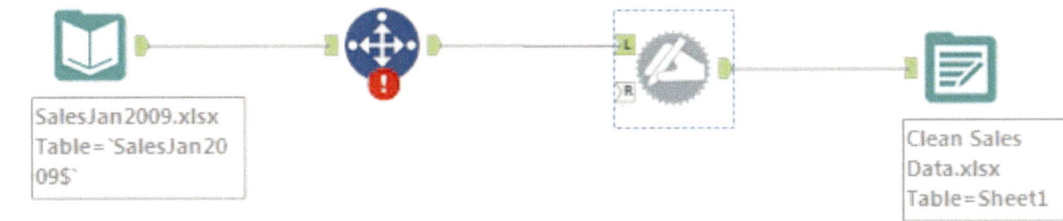

Jlts - Workflow - Messages

① 1 Errors	① 0 Conv Errors	⚠ 0 Warnings	☐ 1 Messages	🖪 1 Files	All

☐	**Designer x64**	**Started running C:\Users\greent2\Desktop\TG Files\Alteryx\5.2 - Out	**
☐	**Designer x64**	The Designer x64 reported: Allocating requested dedicated sort/join memory w
①	Select Records (17)	**Tool #10: Parse Error at char(0): Empty expression**
☐	Input Data (15)	990 records were read from "C:\Users\greent2\Desktop\TG Files\Alteryx\4.3 - S
①	**Designer x64**	**Finished running Output Data.yxmd in 1.7 seconds with 1 error**

- The first error message in red offers a clue in its use of the term "Empty expression."

- When you click on the "Select Records" tool you see the following.
  - First, there is a more simplified view in the Results Window; you only see information on the error.
  - Second, clicking on the tool brings up its configuration window.
    - After looking, you see that the "Ranges" section is blank.
    - Now the "Empty expression" error message makes more sense.
    - In short, the "Ranges" section must be populated or it will trigger an error in the workflow.

Select Records (17) - Configuration   ∨ 🗗   Output Data.yxmd*   ✕   +

Questions

Enter the numeric ranges of records to return. For
Example:

-2
3
17-20
50+

Ranges:

SalesJan2009.xlsx
Table=`SalesJan20
09$`

Tool #10: Parse
Error at char(0):
Empty expression

Results - Select Records (17) - Messages

① 1 Errors	① 0 Conv Errors	⚠ 0 Warnings	☐ 0 Messages	🖪 0 Files	All
①	Select Records (17)	**Tool #10: Parse Error at char(0): Empty expression**			

- After populating the "Ranges" section of the "Select Tools" configuration and re-running the workflow, you hear that satisfying chime that tells you that your workflow is clean and error-free.

- As a final tip, the notes section of the Results Window can get busy with a lot of information.
    - To simplify its presentation, you can click on the "Errors" button see only the error messages created by your workflow.
    - This same "view simplification" concept applies to all the buttons in the Results Window section: Conversion Errors, Warnings, Messages, etc.

The significance of "Warnings"

- By default, errors stop your workflow (until you fix them), but warnings do not.

- Consider a warning as a "heads up" from Alteryx, something that it views as a potential inconsistency in your data or some other item to note.

- As a practical matter, if my output is being transformed as I intended, I don't spend a lot of time looking at or worrying about warnings.

A summary of the other Result Window buttons

- Anchor buttons
    - If you click on the input anchor in the Results Window, you will see a display of the data coming into the selected tool.
    - The same (but opposite) concept applies when you click on the output anchor in the Results Window.

- Messages
    - Clicking on this button will display any messages generated by a tool.

- Data and Metadata
    - When "Data" is highlighted, the results of your data will appear in the Results Widow.
    - "Metadata" is often defined as "data about data."
        - Clicking on this button will display characteristics of the data within a given tool.
        - As an example, referring to the illustration that follows:
            - Name – This contains the name (or description) of the columns (or fields) in your dataset.
            - Type – This describes the data type (or format) of the data in the columns.
                - "V-String" indicates that the columns in this dataset contain text.[12]
            - Size – This is the file size of the data.

---

[12] The concept of "data types" will be covered in detail later.

- Source
  - Remember that Alteryx workflows start out as a blank Canvas; the source data must come from somewhere.
  - The "Metadata" option shows the filepath of the data that's coming into the tool.

Record	Name	Type	Size	Source
1	F2	V_String	255	File: C:\Users
2	F3	V_String	255	File: C:\Users
3	F4	V_String	255	File: C:\Users
4	F5	V_String	255	File: C:\Users

57 of 57 Fields — Cell Viewer —

Sorting and filtering data

- As previously noted, the "perfect way" to evaluate whether your data output is correct is to export it and review it in full.

- However, this can be tedious, time-consuming, and is often unnecessary.

- In most cases, a quick review of the data in the Results Window will tell you if you're on the right track in designing your workflow to meet your needs.

- However, to verify that your data is being organized and handled as you intended, sometimes you need to see it in a more intuitive format than what's presented by default in the Results Window.

- One quick thing you can do to get more insight into your data is to sort it in the Results Window.
  - This is done by clicking on a column's (bolded) field name.

- For example, the default display output in the Results Window is the order of the data as it comes into a given tool (see the illustration that follows).

	Transaction_date	Product	Price	Payment_Type
1	2009-01-02 06:17:00	Product1	1200	Mastercard
2	2009-01-02 04:53:00	Product1	1200	Visa
3	2009-01-02 13:08:00	Product1	1200	Mastercard
4	2009-01-03 14:44:00	Product1	1200	Visa
5	2009-01-04 12:56:00	Product2	3600	Visa

- However, if we want to see the output displayed by "Payment_Type" then:
  - Move the cursor over "Payment_Type" in the Results Window.
  - Click on the symbol with the three dots to the right.

- Click on the up arrow to sort the data in ascending (or alphabetical) order.
  - For numbers, sorting in ascending order will display small numbers first and work up to larger ones.
- Now the output will look like this (notice that "Amex" transactions now appear first).

	Transaction_date	Product	Price	Payment_Type
1	2009-01-05 05:39:00	Product1	1200	Amex
2	2009-01-06 07:46:00	Product1	1200	Amex
3	2009-01-06 22:19:00	Product2	3600	Amex
4	2009-01-06 23:00:00	Product2	3600	Amex
5	2009-01-07 20:15:00	Product1	1200	Amex

- In addition to *sorting* data as described above, you can *filter* it.
  - For example, if you only wanted to see Visa transactions then you could type "Visa" in the "Filter" section.

- Click the "X" within the "Sort/Filter" section to remove the sorting and/or filtering of your data in the Results Window.

- Other items to note:
  - If you re-run your workflow then all sorting and filtering will be removed.
  - Sorting and filtering only affects what you see in the Results Window; it does *not* impact your source or output data.
  - If you need to see more results than what's displayed on the screen, you can use the scroll button at the far right of the Results Window to navigate further down.

6.6 A Greater Depth of Knowledge Allows You to Keep it Simple

In general

- Before moving on to more tools, I want to emphasize that "more" does not necessarily mean "better."
  - In fact, keeping it simple is often *vastly* more effective.

- There are many, MANY examples where this principle applies, but I'll share just a few.

A baseball analogy

- Question – What pitch do major league pitchers throw to hitters (the best hitters in the world) the most?

- Statistics vary over time, but it's estimated that some variant of a fastball is thrown by pitchers about 60% of the time.
  - For power pitchers – those who dominate the game – the percentage can be much higher.
- Interestingly, the only player ever unanimously elected to the Baseball Hall of Fame was Mariano Rivera, a relief pitcher who essentially threw ONE PITCH.
  - It was a cut fastball.
  - Everyone he faced knew it was coming.
  - Despite this, Rivera threw his bread and butter pitch to such perfection that players still found it almost impossible to hit.

- The point here is that casual observers of the game of baseball often believe it's the number of pitches in a player's arsenal that that makes the difference. In reality:
  - It's not how many pitches you throw, it's how well you throw the pitches that you know.

- Alteryx is very similar.
  - Don't think it's the total number of tools you know that makes the difference.
  - Yes, just like a pitcher needs to hit a certain velocity for their fastball to be effective, you need to know a certain number of Alteryx tools to tackle a solid variety of accounting, tax, and finance data-related challenges.
  - BUT once you've been introduced to enough tools to fill a basic toolkit:
    - It's how well you know and apply them verses the sheer number of tools that you use in a workflow that wins the day.
  - And finally, like a fastball, some of the most _powerful_ tools in Alteryx are the _easiest_ to use and understand.
    - Something doesn't have to be complicated to be effective.

The Theory of Relativity

- As another "keep it simple" analogy, it's astonishing to me that Albert Einstein had the intellectual capacity and creativity to develop the Theory of Relativity.

- However, Einstein's genius didn't stop there. He had the clarity of thought to distill his understanding of this astonishingly complex concept down to this:

$$E = mc^2$$

- Now THAT'S taking something complicated and presenting it in a simple way!

The challenges of applying the concept of simplicity to Alteryx

Following are the reasons I see workflows get out-of-hand complicated.

1) **Lack of Understanding** – When users don't have a sufficient depth of understanding of how tools work, they end up using even more tools to compensate.
   a. "I need a tool to get my data to go to the left."
   b. "Whoa! That's TOO far to the left. Let me use another tool to push the data back to the right."
   c. "Hmmm, that's still not what I'm looking for. I'll just use another tool to fix the problem..."

2) **Lack of Clarity** – Having clarity means knowing exactly what you're trying to accomplish and having a clear vision of how to get there.
   a. I'm not suggesting that you need to have every tool mapped out in your mind (or on paper) before starting a workflow.
   b. What I am suggesting is that your workflows are going to get messy if you just wing it, importing data and manipulating it without thinking through the progression of goals you need to meet along the way to successfully create your output.

3) **Not Going the Distance** – Even with the best of intentions:
   a. You may not have enough knowledge or experience with Alteryx tools to use them how you need to without some experimentation.
   b. You may also need to try different workflow configurations before you're able to visualize what's necessary to accomplish your data-related goals.
   c. This kind of experimentation – splashing different things on your Canvas – can get a bit messy.
      i. That's okay – many times that's what it takes to solve complex problems.
   d. However, after you develop a clear picture of how to design and configure your workflow, put in the effort to make your workflow as simple as possible.
      i. If you do, you'll make it _much easier_ for you and others to use, follow, test, modify and build on your work.
      ii. If you don't, no matter how much effort and brainpower goes into your workflow, its complexity will limit its usefulness.

- While my advice to keep workflow simple sounds easy, in practice it takes a lot of thought, knowledge, effort and tradecraft to create a workflow that resembles something like "$E = mc^2$."

- On the other hand, if you don't follow my advice, you could have workflows that look like the one that follows (yes, it's real, and it's not even the entire workflow!).

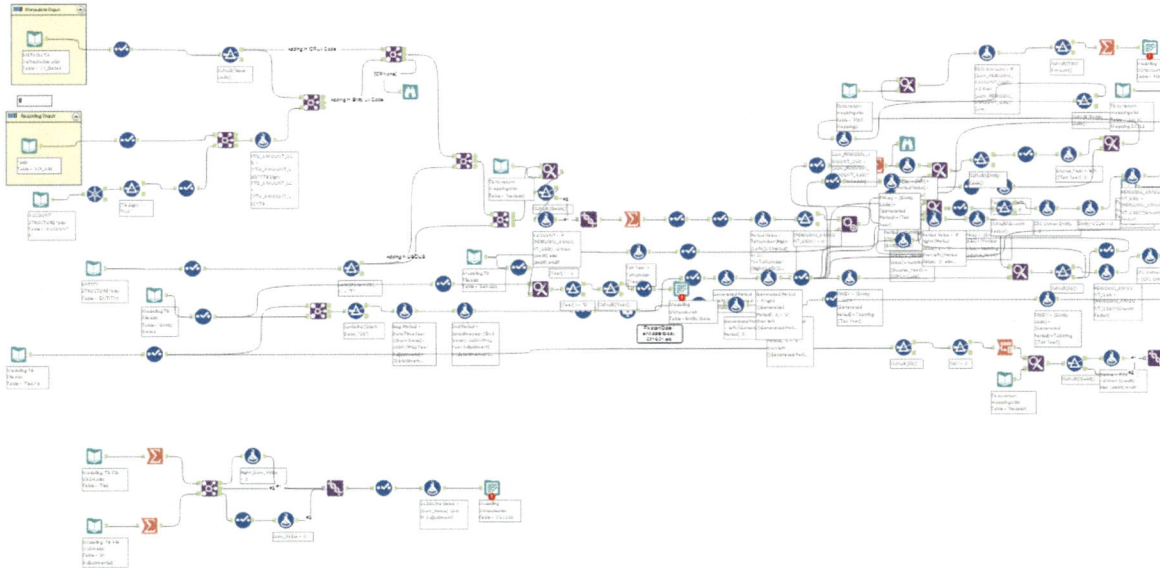

6.7 Summarizing Your Progress and Where You Go from Here

Here is where we are now:

1) You have a good handle on Alteryx terminology and concepts.
2) You know how to import data into Alteryx.
3) Using Alteryx tools, you've mastered how to organize and streamline the top section of your data.
4) You've completed you're first workflow, and you've successfully exported the data it produced to a separate Excel file.
5) You have a deeper understanding of Alteryx's screen layout, as well as how to evaluate your data as it travels through your workflow.
6) You recognize the importance of honing your knowledge and application of a targeted set of Alteryx tools so that you can use them effectively while keeping your workflows clean, efficient, and organized.

By following this pattern, you're now ready to take your use of Alteryx to the next level. So, get back to Han Solo and tell him that you're ready for the jump to hyperspace!

7 Use the "Select" Tool to Organize and Format Columns

7.1 Learning Objectives

Upon the completion of this chapter, you will:

- Know how to use the "Select" tool to rename, reorder, delete and format columns.
- Recognize what Alteryx "data types" are, how they impact your data, and how you can use the "Select" tool to change them to meet your needs.
- Understand where to strategically place "Select" tools in your workflows and why it's important.

7.2 An Introduction to the "Select" Tool

- In this chapter we will continue with the theme of using Alteryx to organize messy data in a format that it can be immediately integrated into Excel (or other) calculations.
  - o In this case, "immediately" means "immediately."
  - o In other words, we don't want to export data to Excel only to have to do further manual modifications so we can *finally* do our calculations!

- "Select" is a powerful tool that helps to accomplish this goal.
  - o In fact, the "Select" tool is so useful that's it's rare to see a workflow without one.

- Fundamentally, the purpose of the "Select" tool is to organize and format the *fields* (or columns) of the data in a workflow.
  - o The "Select" tool is NOT used to manage or edit rows.
  - o For that – editing rows – we'll use the "Filter" tool, which will be covered later.

- As we walk through the "Select" tool, we'll build on the workflow we created earlier to organize sales data.

SalesJan2009.xlsx
Table=`SalesJan20
09$`

Clean Sales
Data.xlsx
Table=Sheet1

7.3   How to Rename Columns

- To get started, the first thing we want to do is to rename the first column.
  - Specifically, we want to change its name from "Transaction_date" to "Transaction Date" before the data is exported to Excel by the "Output Data" tool.

	Transaction_date	Product	Price
1	2009-01-02 06:17:00	Product1	1200
2	2009-01-02 04:53:00	Product1	1200
3	2009-01-02 13:08:00	Product1	1200

- The first step is to accomplish this is to drag a "Select" tool to the Canvas.
  - Place it after "Dynamic Rename" and before "Output Data" (as shown below)
  - After doing so, our workflow will look like this.

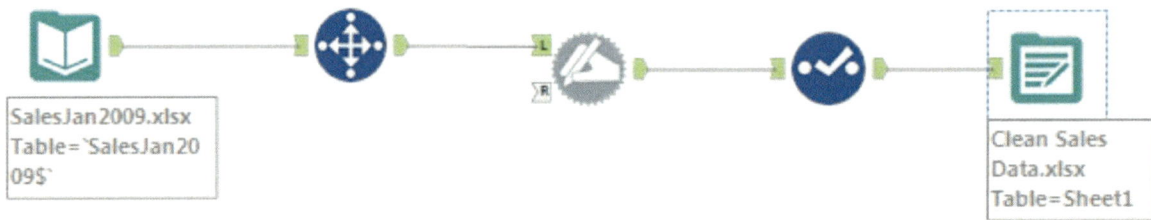

SalesJan2009.xlsx
Table=`SalesJan20
09$`

Clean Sales
Data.xlsx
Table=Sheet1

- After clicking on the "Select" tool to configure it, we'll see something like this.

Options ▾ | ↑ ↓   TIP: To reorder multiple rows: select, right-click and drag.

	Field	Type	Size	Rename	Description
☑	Transaction_date	V_String	255		
☑	Product	V_String	255		
☑	Price	V_String	255		
☑	Payment_Type	V_String	255		
☑	Name	V_String	255		
☑	City	V_String	255		
☑	State	V_String	255		
☑	Country	V_String	255		
☑	Account_Created	V_String	255		
☑	Last_Login	V_String	255		
☑	Latitude	V_String	255		
☑	Longitude	V_String	255		
☑	*Unknown	Unknown	0		Dynamic or Unkno...

- In the "Rename" column type "Transaction Date," as shown below.

	Field	Type		Size	Rename	Description
✓	Transaction_date	V_String	▾	255	Transaction Date	

- After doing this, notice the names of other columns that need be cleaned up as well. We can follow the same approach described above to make the following changes:
  - "Price" to "Sales Price."
  - "Payment_type" to "Credit Card."
  - "Account_Created" to "Date Account Created."
  - "Last_Login" to "Last Login."

- After re-running the workflow, we will see our changes in the column headings reflected as follows.

	Transaction Date	Product	Price	Credit Card
1	2009-01-02 06:17:00	Product1	1200	Mastercard
2	2009-01-02 04:53:00	Product1	1200	Visa
3	2009-01-02 13:08:00	Product1	1200	Mastercard

7.4 How to Delete Columns

- For our purposes, we've decided that we don't need the "Name," "Latitude" and "Longitude" columns in our final dataset to be exported to Excel.

- To remove these columns, uncheck the boxes for those fields.

Options ▾ | ↑ ↓   TIP: To reorder multiple rows: select, right-click and drag.

	Field	Type		Size	Rename	Description
✓	Transaction_date	V_String	▾	255	Transaction Date	
✓	Product	V_String	▾	255		
✓	Price	V_String	▾	255	Sales Price	
✓	Payment_Type	V_String	▾	255	Credit Card	
☐	Name	V_String	▾	255		
✓	City	V_String	▾	255		
✓	State	V_String	▾	255		
✓	Country	V_String	▾	255		
✓	Account_Created	V_String	▾	255	Date Account Created	
✓	Last_Login	V_String	▾	255	Last Login	
☐	Latitude	V_String	▾	255		
☐	Longitude	V_String	▾	255		

- After re-running your workflow, the unchecked columns will be removed from the output.

7.5   How to Reorder Columns

- For our output, we decide the ordering of the columns needs to be changed from:
  - City-State-Country to
  - Country-State-City.

- To do this, click on the "Country" line in the "Select" tool's configuration (see the blue row highlighted in the illustration below).
  - After that, click on the up arrow (to the right of "Options") until the "Country" line is positioned above "City."
  - From there, click on the "City" line, and then click the down arrow to move "City" below "State."

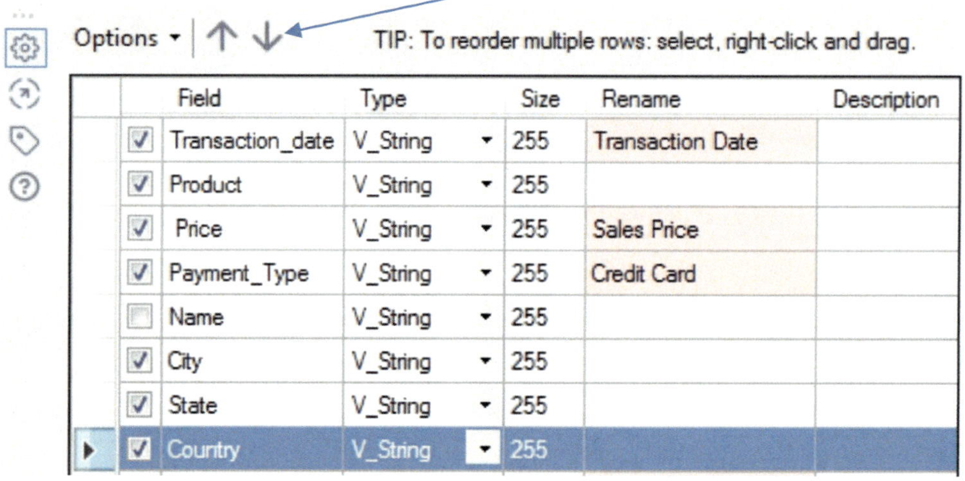

- After we're done, the configuration should look like this (Country, State, and City in sequential order).

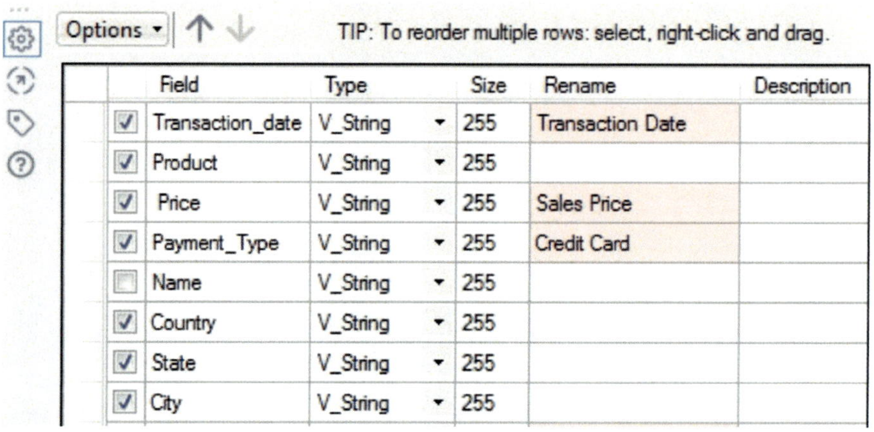

- After re-running the workflow, the columns will be reordered as shown below.

Transaction Date	Product	Sales Price	Credit Card	Country	State	City
1 2009-01-02 06:17:00	Product1	1200	Mastercard	United Kingdom	England	Basildon
2 2009-01-02 04:53:00	Product1	1200	Visa	United States	MO	Parkville
3 2009-01-02 13:08:00	Product1	1200	Mastercard	United States	OR	Astoria
4 2009-01-03 14:44:00	Product1	1200	Visa	Australia	Victoria	Echuca

7.6 An Introduction to Alteryx "Data Types" and using the "Select" Tool to Change Them

An example of when the wrong "data type" causes a problem

- While there are certain data types in Alteryx that you'll never use or care about, data types is NOT a subject that accounting, tax, and finance professionals can ignore.

- To illustrate how data types can impact your output, we'll continue with our sales data example and assume the following:
  - o We've exported what we thought was cleaned up data from Alteryx to an Excel file.
  - o In Excel, we now need to sum the amounts in the "Sales Price" column to support other calculations (see the illustration below).
  - o To accomplish this in Excel we:
    - Navigate to the bottom of the "Sales Price" column.
    - Click the "Sum" button.
    - Select cells A2-A986.
    - Click "Enter" and
    - Excel computes the total to be…zero?

	A	B	C	D
1	Transaction Date	Product	Sales Price	Credit Card
983	2009-01-26 11:19:00	Product1	1200	Mastercard
984	2009-01-05 13:23:00	Product1	1200	Visa
985	2009-01-28 05:36:00	Product2	3600	Visa
986	2009-01-01 04:24:00	Product3	7500	Amex
987				
988	Total Sales		0	

- What's going on? Why is Excel returning a zero value when summing a column of numbers?
  - o The answer is that Excel is NOT treating the figures in the "Sales Price" column as numbers, but as TEXT.

- To understand why, it's important to learn something about Alteryx data types.
  - As I alluded to earlier, the purpose of the following is not to cover ALL Alteryx data types, only the ones that are the most relevant for accounting, tax, and finance professionals.

Alteryx data types in general

- "Data types" govern how Alteryx treats data in a specific column (or "field").

- When data is imported into Alteryx using an "Input Data" tool it's automatically assigned a data type.

- If you need to change the data type for a column (or field), you can easily do so using the "Select" tool as we will see shortly.

- The data types accounting, tax, and finance professionals care about fall into three categories:
  - Numbers
  - Text and
  - Dates.

- A summary of each of these data types is covered in the subsections that follow.

Numeric data

- Numeric data types are quantitative in nature, meaning they can be measured (e.g., in numbers, dollars, miles, etc.) and used in computations.

- Following are common choices for data types.[13]

  1) Double – Use this data type to preserve decimals in your output, i.e., to <u>avoid</u> rounding.
     a. 3.1415 vs. "3."
     b. I use "Double" more than any other numeric data type because it preserves all values/figures in their original state.

  2) Int32 – Use this data type to round figures to whole numbers.
     a. Whole numbers will be output; the exact unrounded number will be lost (but will still be in your original source data file).
     b. You can use this setting when, for example, you want to drop cents from financial amounts.
     c. A zip code is another example where you might use Int32 since Zip codes are not rounded.

---

[13] And, no, I'm not sure why data types have such non-intuitive names.

3) Fixed ("Fixed Decimal") – Unfortunately, despite what the name of this data type implies, it does NOT round figures to the decimal place you want.
   a. For example, rounding the decimal place of financial figures two places to capture cents.
   b. As a result, I don't find this data type to be useful.

- The bottom line is if you want the data in a column (or field) to be treated as numbers, *it's hard to go wrong with the "Double" data type.*

String (or "text") data

- String data is "Alteryx-speak" for data in a text format.
  o String data is used for *organization* and NOT for computations.

- Examples of columns (or fields) that should have string data types are as follows:
  o Entity names
  o Account names
  o Descriptions or explanations.

- What about a column with account numbers? Should it be coded as a number or as a string (text)?
  o In my opinion, since an account number is an identifier (and NOT used for counting or measuring), it should be coded as a string.

- There are two common string data types.

1) Variable ("V_String") – This is data where the description varies in length.
   a. The name of an entity would be an example, since some entity names are short, and others are long.
   b. This is the most flexible and accommodating string (or text) data type.

2) Fixed – This is data that has the same number of characters.
   a. An account number would be an example (assuming they all have the same number of digits).

- If a column contains text then, for accounting, tax, and finance professionals, *it's hard to go wrong with the "V_String" data type.*

Time and date-related data types

- This is data that has to do with time: years, months, the time of day, and so on.

- Selecting a time-related data type is necessary for a given column if you want to do computations that measure time.
  o How many days is it between one accounting period and another?

- How much time did a product spend in inventory until it was shipped, and so on?

- Your data type choices for measuring time are as follows:
  - Date – This processes data in the format "yyyy-mm-dd."
  - Time – The format for this data type is "hh:mm:ss."
  - DateTime – This is a combination of both: "yyyy-mm-dd hh:mm:ss."

- If a column contains time-related data then *"Date" is the most common selection for accounting, tax, and finance professionals*.

Use the "Select" tool to choose the appropriate data type for a column

- Now that you know how data types impact the way Alteryx reads and outputs your data, it's time to dive into the "Select" tool's configuration to fix the "Sales Price" column.

- First, click on the "Select" tool to bring up its configuration.
  - The illustration below shows all the fields (or columns) in your data.
  - And, yes, it's a bit disorienting, unusual, and even a bit ironic that your *columns* are presented as *rows* in the "Select" tool's configuration!

Options ▾ ↑ ↓   TIP: To reorder multiple rows: select, right-click and drag.

	Field	Type		Size	Rename	Description
☑	Transaction_date	V_String	▾	255	Transaction Date	
☑	Product	V_String	▾	255		
☑	Price	V_String	▾	255	Sales Price	
☑	Payment_Type	V_String	▾	255	Credit Card	
☐	Name	V_String	▾	255		
☑	Country	V_String	▾	255		
☑	State	V_String	▾	255		
☑	City	V_String	▾	255		
☑	Account_Created	V_String	▾	255	Date Account Created	
☑	Last_Login	V_String	▾	255	Last Login	
☐	Latitude	V_String	▾	255		
☐	Longitude	V_String	▾	255		

- Notice that the "Sales Price" field (or column) is categorized as a "V-String."
  - This is what's causing Alteryx to treat the figures in that column as text, which is why Excel is reading the data in that column as text.

- To fix the issue, click on the down-arrow by "V-String" in the "Type" column and select "Double" as the new data type.

	Field	Type		Size	Rename
✓	Transaction_date	V_String	▾	255	Transaction Date
✓	Product	V_String	▾	255	
✓	Price	Double	▾	8	Sales Price

- After you re-run the workflow, you can open the "Clean Sales Data" file in Excel, sum the figures in the "Sales Price" column, and you will get the following result.

1	Transaction Date	Product	Sales Price	Credit Card
984	2009-01-05 13:23:00	Product1	1200	Visa
985	2009-01-28 05:36:00	Product2	3600	Visa
986	2009-01-01 04:24:00	Product3	7500	Amex
987				
988	Total Sales		1612500	

- Now that you've confirmed that Excel is reading the data in the "Sales Price" column as numbers, you can complete whatever calculations you need.

- In summary, the "Select" tool gives you an extraordinary amount of control over how Alteryx (and Excel) read and process your data.

7.7 Use the "Select" Tool at the Beginning and the End of Your Workflows

The "why" behind the importance of developing clean workflows

- If you haven't figured it out already, then you'll know soon enough that there are often many ways to design and configure a workflow to address the same data-related goals and challenges.

- That said, it's important as a reader for you to recognize that I've got some strong biases when it comes to working with Alteryx (and Excel as well…but that's a story for another day).
    - One of those biases, which I've already touched on, is that I'm strongly in favor of clean, efficient, and well-organized workflows.
    - A second (and related) bias is that I believe *a workflow's design should favor what's easier for someone else to review* vs. what's faster, easier, and more convenient for a designer to prepare.

- With that in mind, let me express these same biases in terms of what I am NOT in favor of.

- I'm not in favor of messy, convoluted, and disorganized workflows that use a million tools and meander all over the place, *even if they eventually get to the right answer*.
    - In short, just because the Alteryx workspace is a "Canvas" doesn't mean you can haphazardly splash whatever tools you want on there and I'm going to call it art.
    - To sum up, I don't care how brilliant you are, I don't care what level of knowledge went into creating your workflow, and it doesn't matter to me what level of sophistication you applied in selecting and configuring the tools in your workflow…
    - If I can't follow what's going on – if I can't follow your work in a logical progression from beginning to end – then, speaking as a reviewer, your work is practically useless as far as I'm concerned.

- Here's the bottom line. As accounting, tax, and finance professionals, it's not enough to just get "the right answer."
    - People are counting on our work to make material financial decisions that affect their businesses, their careers, and even their lives.
    - Given that so much is on the line, we owe it to those who review our work to not only give them correct information, but to present it in a manner that helps them get comfortable with *why* it's right and *how we got there*.

Use the "Select" tool near the beginning and end of workflows

- Consistent with the principles above, using the "Select" tool near the beginning of a workflow can markedly simplify your work.

- For example, let's say that the raw data you import into your workflow has 100 columns, but only 10 of them are relevant for your calculations.
    - By using the "Select" tool early on to eliminate the 90 unnecessary columns, you make it far easier for you and others to follow what's going on in your workflow.

- I also find it helpful to use the "Select" tool near the end of a workflow, because it provides an opportunity to do a final clean-up of data before it's exported to Excel.

Other items to note on the use the "Select" tool

- I recommend that you only use the "Select" tool to format your data.
    - Why do I say this? It's because there are other tools that also give you the option to format field (or column) data.
    - The "Join" tool, which we'll cover later, is one example.

- What's wrong with formatting data with other tools besides "Select?"
    - There's nothing "wrong" with it in terms of getting to the correct answer.

- However, remember what we covered earlier in terms of making your workflows as logical and easy to review as possible.
    - While you CAN format data using other tools, that's not what a reviewer is necessarily looking for or expecting.
    - If, instead, you discipline yourself to exclusively use the "Select" tool to format data then it will make your workflows more intuitive and easier to use, review, update, and adapt to other uses.

- Finally, while I believe that it's a good practice to have "Select" tools near the beginning and the end of your workflows, you should consider that as guidance and not as a limitation.
    - In short, place "Select" tools in your workflows as they're needed, but in doing so try to keep your workflows as simple, organized, and as logically constructed as possible.

8 Use the "Filter" to Clean Up and Extract Data Organized in Rows

8.1 Learning Objectives

Upon the completion of this chapter, you will:

- Learn the differences between the "Filter" tool and the "Select Records" tool in how they impact row of data.
- Know how to use the "Filter" tool to manage rows in the main body of your data, as well as why it's far more efficient than using the "Select Records" tool to do so.
- Be able to use the "Filter" tool to isolate or remove targeted rows of data from your dataset.
- Differentiate between static and dynamic approaches to resolving data-related challenges, and the positive impact this can have on Excel-based work products.

8.2 An Introduction to the "Filter" Tool

For the "Select" tool think "columns," and for the "Filter" tool think "rows"

- While the "Select" tool is extremely effective at cleaning up columns, it has _zero impact_ on rows.

- Instead, you need the "Filter" tool to clean up and extract data in rows.

An example of data-related problems with rows

- As we've been working with sales data in examples up to this point, we've assumed that the rows have been clean and orderly.
    - With raw financial data, this is often the _exception_ more than the rule!
    - For example, what if your sales data contains numerous instances of breaks in rows like the one shown in the illustration that follows?

[This space was intentionally left blank].

◢	A	B	C	D	E
1	**Sales Report for Company X**				
2	**Period: Q1 2021**				
3					
4					
5	Transaction_date	Product	Price	Payment_Type	Name	City
97	1/3/2009 13:56	Product1	1,200	Visa	Rennae	Amelia Island
98	1/4/2009 7:54	Product1	1,200	Visa	Gerhard	Alliston
99	1/12/2009 7:28	Product1	1,200	Amex	Megan	La Alberca
100	This is an artifical break in the data.				
101					
102					
103					
104					
105	1/6/2009 15:15	Product1	1,200	Mastercard	Danielle	Rathgar
106	1/13/2009 23:56	Product1	1,200	Mastercard	Tod	Coral Gables
107	1/14/2009 19:32	Product1	1,200	Visa	Janaina	Miami
108	1/6/2009 21:13	Product1	1,200	Visa	Kofi	Vancouver

- Referring to row 100 in the raw Excel file above:
  - In our example it says, "This is an artificial break in the data."
  - It could just as easily say something like "Page 3" (followed by pages 4, 5, 6, etc.).
  - Also note the blank rows 101-104.
  - Finally, assume all these issues exist in the raw data because that's how it comes out of your company's ERP system.

- If we don't remove these gaps in our data, it will disrupt our Excel calculations.
  - When that happens, we could manually fix everything using Excel.
  - However, a far more efficient approach is to use Alteryx's "Filter" tool to clean up our rows before we export our data to Excel.

8.3   Why "Select Records" is NOT the Best Tool to Manage Rows in the Main Body of Data

The "Select Records" tool is also used to manage rows

- Using the "Filter" is an excellent way to remove unneeded rows from the main body a dataset.

- But why? Can't we use "Select Records" instead, as opposed to having to learn about and rely on another tool?
  - In a Chapter 4 example, we used "5+" in the "Select Records" configuration to skip over the first four rows and to show the remaining data starting with row five.

- - Can't we just as easily address our problem in the present example by using the following in our "Select Records" configuration?
    - 5-99
    - 105+

- This *will* work in the sense that it will fix the problem *that we can see* in the "Sales Report" illustration on the previous page. Specifically, it will:
  - Remove the first four rows of data (that we don't want) and start with row 5.
  - It will also eliminate rows 100-104 (which we also don't want), effectively "sewing" the data that we want together in a string of continuous rows.

Using "Select Records" to manage rows has shortcomings

- However, using "Select Records" to address the example presented at the beginning of this chapter has serious shortcomings because it's a *manual process*.
  - In other words, the "Select Records" tool works fine if you only have one instance of breaks in your rows.
  - But what if this dataset contains *40,000* lines and it's got *400* different breaks in the rows.
  - If that's the case, using "Select Records" would be an incredibly time-consuming way to address the problem.
    - Call me crazy, but I believe that a desire to employ this kind of mind-numbing manual approach isn't why you've come this far in your efforts to learn Alteryx.
    - In addition, I'll take another leap and guess that you didn't become an accounting, tax, or finance professional because the idea of manually manipulating data excited you so much!

- Continuing with the previous point, the problem with using the "Select Records" tool to address the present example is that it's a "static" rather than a "dynamic" solution.
  - A static approach is one where Alteryx will follow your commands to the letter, not adjusting to changes and alterations in your underlying data.
  - For example, if you configure the "Select Records" tool to skip over rows 100-104 in your raw data, that's what Designer will do…period.
  - This might be fine if the structure of your source data never changes or if you have a small dataset, but what if the ERP system shifts 40,000 lines of data you need to analyze down by one row?
  - If the format of your raw data changes, then it means all the time and effort you put into manually formatting the "Select Records" tool went up in flames, and you'll have to start from scratch to ensure that your data output is correct.
    - Ahhhhhhhhhhhhhhhh!! ☹

- In summary, yes, it's true that the "Select Records" tool is the best way to manage rows at the TOP of a dataset.
  - However, because its configuration is static (vs. dynamic) in nature, it's a blunt tool for managing rows in the main body of a dataset.

o There is a vastly better way to address row-related issues such as the one described above, and it's by using the "Filter" tool.

8.4 Use the "Filter" Tool to Eliminate Unneeded Rows from a Dataset[14]

Some background for understanding how to use the "Filter" tool effectively

- To remove unneeded rows from our data, we'll first drag a "Filter" tool to the Canvas.
    - o After doing so, our workflow will look like this.
    - o Note: The "Filter" tool has a red exclamation point to remind us that it needs to be configured before the workflow will run (or we'll trigger an error).

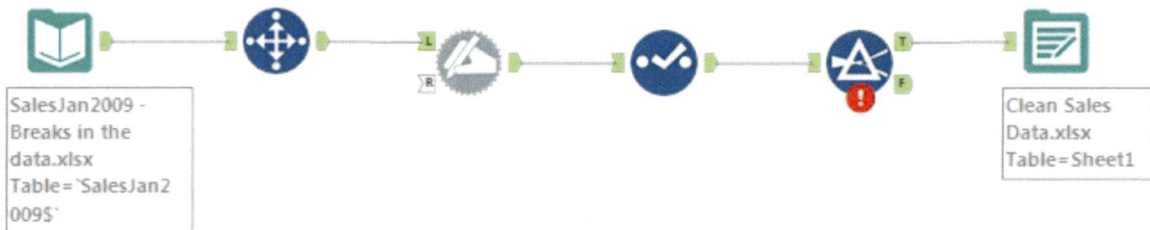

SalesJan2009 -
Breaks in the
data.xlsx
Table=`SalesJan2
009$`

Clean Sales
Data.xlsx
Table=Sheet1

- To better understand how to configure the "Filter" tool, it will help to click on its input anchor to view the data as it comes into it.
    - o If we go to the Results Window and scroll down to line 95, we see the break in the data from the ERP system output we identified earlier.

	Transaction Date	Product	Sales Price	Credit Card
93	2009-01-04 07:54:00	Product1	1200	Visa
94	2009-01-12 07:28:00	Product1	1200	Amex
95	This is an artifical break i...	[Null]	[Null]	[Null]
96	[Null]	[Null]	[Null]	[Null]
97	[Null]	[Null]	[Null]	[Null]
98	[Null]	[Null]	[Null]	[Null]
99	[Null]	[Null]	[Null]	[Null]
100	2009-01-06 15:15:00	Product1	1200	Mastercard
101	2009-01-13 23:56:00	Product1	1200	Mastercard

- o We'll assume there are other breaks in the data as well; lines 95-99 are not the only ones.

---

[14] The "Summarize" tool also offers powerful ways to manage data in rows. This will be covered in Chapter 12.

- This means any (ideal) filtering solution needs to address ALL breaks in the data, not just the ones we see in the illustration.
  - o In addition, note that the empty cells are not just blank; Alteryx has assigned each the value of "[Null]."
  - o With these observations in mind, we're now ready to configure the "Filter" tool.

Configuring the "Filter" tool

- Click on the "Filter" tool in the workflow to open its configuration.

- From there:
  - o Click on "Basic filter."
  - o Click on the field (or column) on which you want to apply your filter.
    - This is a CRITICAL concept, namely that the "Filter" tool impacts ROWS, but it filters those rows based on the data it evaluates in the specific COLUMN that you choose.
  - o Choose "Credit Card" as the column (or field) you want to filter on in the dropdown menu.
    - Following the reasoning above, we're telling the "Filter" tool to separate out ROWS based on what it sees in the "Credit Card" column.
  - o Select "Is not null" for the final filter criteria.

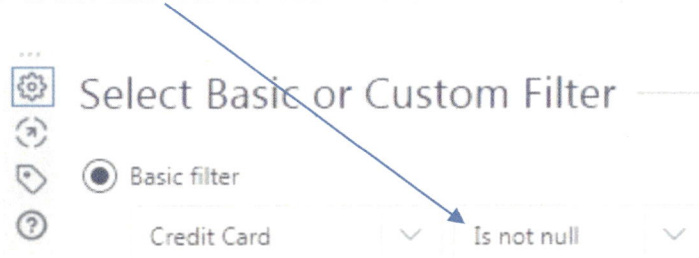

- After taking all these steps, we're ready to run the workflow.

An overview of how the "Filter" tool works

- Pulling all the above concepts together, you've configured the "Filter" tool to do the following:
  - o Scan the "Credit Card" column.
  - o In any instance where Alteryx encounters credit card data (such as Mastercard, Visa, etc.), these rows will be processed as "True" data that will flow to the "Filter" tool's "T" output anchor.
  - o If data does NOT meet the filter criteria (meaning it's "[Null]"), Alteryx will remove the ENTIRE ROW from the dataset and send it to the "Filter" tool's false (of "F") output anchor.
    - See what the "F" output looks like in the illustration below.

	Transaction Date	Product	Sales Price	Credit Card
1	This is an artifical break in the data.	[Null]	[Null]	[Null]
2	[Null]	[Null]	[Null]	[Null]
3	[Null]	[Null]	[Null]	[Null]
4	[Null]	[Null]	[Null]	[Null]
5	[Null]	[Null]	[Null]	[Null]
6	This is another artifical break in the data	[Null]	[Null]	[Null]
7	[Null]	[Null]	[Null]	[Null]
8	[Null]	[Null]	[Null]	[Null]

- Taking a step back, do you see what we've done?
  - We recognized in looking at the raw data that any row that contained "null" data was one that we didn't need or want.
  - We also noticed that if a cell in the "Credit Card" column was "null," the entire row should be pulled out from our final data.
  - Following this logic, the "Filter" tool removed all extraneous rows from the data.
    - We would have gotten the same successful result had we filtered on the columns (or fields) "Product" or "Sales Price."
    - However, filtering on "Transaction Date" would NOT have worked.
      - This is because some rows in this column are NOT "null."
      - Instead, they contain text ("This is an artificial break in the data").

- Below you can see the clean, filtered data that flowed to the "Filter" tool's "true" (or "T") output anchor (noting that all breaks in rows have been removed).

	Transaction Date	Product	Sales Price	Credit Card
91	2009-01-06 17:15:00	Product1	1200	Visa
92	2009-01-03 13:56:00	Product1	1200	Visa
93	2009-01-04 07:54:00	Product1	1200	Visa
94	2009-01-12 07:28:00	Product1	1200	Amex
95	2009-01-06 15:15:00	Product1	1200	Mastercard
96	2009-01-13 23:56:00	Product1	1200	Mastercard
97	2009-01-14 19:32:00	Product1	1200	Visa
98	2009-01-06 21:13:00	Product1	1200	Visa
99	2009-01-14 11:19:00	Product1	1200	Visa
100	2009-01-13 19:39:00	Product1	1200	Visa

- As a final observation, note that we've used the "Filter" tool to create a dynamic solution to cleaning up our data.
  - In other words, our "Filtering" tool works according to logic we've configured that will flexibly adapt to any changes that might occur in the underlying data.

8.5   Use the "Filter" Tool to Extract Targeted Sets of Data

Use the "Filter" tool to pare down your data to only what you need

- The "Filter" tool is not only useful for removing extraneous rows, but it can also be used to *extract targeted data*.

- For example, thus far we have been looking at the total population of our sales data.
    - What if we wanted, instead, to only review "Visa" transactions?
    - The "Filter" tool is perfect for this.

An example of using the "Filter" tool to extract data

- To get started, we would drag another "Filter" tool to the Canvas and place it after the one we used to clean up the unnecessary rows.[15]
    - Note that the input anchor of our new "Filter" tool is connected to the "T" output anchor of the first "Filter" tool.
    - This is because we want the cleaned-up sales data flowing into the second "Filter" tool, not the "null" rows that were filtered out and directed to the "F" output.

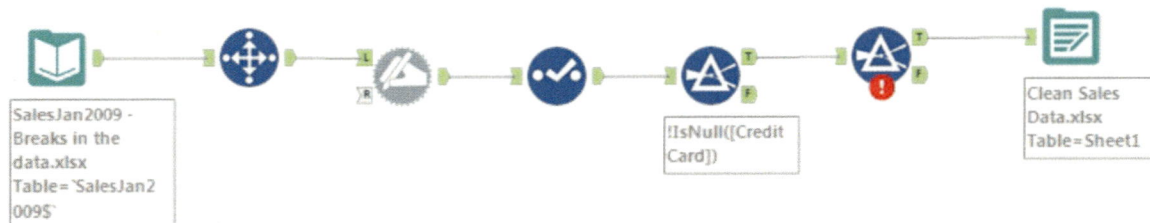

- To configure the tool as show in the illustration that follows, click on the second "Filter" tool and select:
    - "Basic filter."
    - "Credit Card" as the column to evaluate
    - Select "Equals" as the filter criteria and
    - Type "Visa" as the credit card category that you want to filter.
        - This is noteworthy, the fact that you can type a specific term in the filter box such as "Visa," "United States," "Account 100145," etc.

---

[15] It's noteworthy that we're using the same tool twice in a row. In this instance we're applying a progressive filtering technique, performing a preliminary scrub of our data before paring it down even further. This same approach can be taken with other tools, meaning Alteryx doesn't prevent you from using the same tool twice in a row if it makes sense to do so.

    o After running the workflow, all "Visa" transactions will flow to the "T" (or "True") output anchor (pictured below), and all other credit card transactions will be filtered to the "F" (or "False") output anchor.

	Transaction Date	Product	Sales Price	Credit Card
1	2009-01-02 04:53:00	Product1	1200	Visa
2	2009-01-03 14:44:00	Product1	1200	Visa
3	2009-01-04 12:56:00	Product2	3600	Visa
4	2009-01-04 13:19:00	Product1	1200	Visa
5	2009-01-04 14:11:00	Product1	1200	Visa
6	2009-01-05 10:08:00	Product1	1200	Visa

- As a final step, make sure the "Filter" tool's "T" output anchor is connected to your "Output Data" tool, because you only want Visa transactions to export to your Excel file for further calculations and analysis.

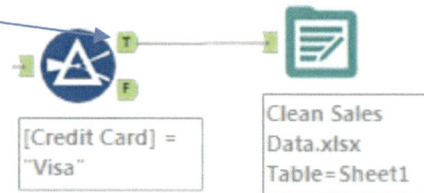

[Credit Card] = "Visa"

Clean Sales Data.xlsx Table=Sheet1

8.6   Other Filter Criteria

- Following the same approach as outlined in the previous section, you can use the "Basic filter" to apply other filtering criteria to your data as well.[16]

- Your "Basic filter" options are as follows:
  - o   Equals (illustrated above in the "Visa" example)
  - o   Does not equal
  - o   Comes before (<)
  - o   Comes after(>)
  - o   Contains
  - o   Does not contain
  - o   Is null
  - o   Is not null
  - o   Is empty
  - o   Is not empty

- Remember, rows that contain data that meet your defined criteria will flow to the "T" output anchor, and all other data will be filtered and flow to the "F" output anchor.

---

[16] The "Custom Filter" section of the configuration can be used to do even more sophisticated filtering, but that requires the use of Alteryx expressions (analogous to formulas in Excel), and that's beyond the scope of this introductory material.

- It's most common to connect the next tool in a workflow to the "Filter's" output anchor ("T").
- That said, there is nothing preventing you from using the filtered data flowing to the "F" output anchor in other parts of your workflow.

8.7 Alteryx Workflows are Dynamic

The problems with manual (static) approaches in working with data

- How would you normally manage a raw, messy dataset using Excel?
  - As previously discussed, the general approach is to save your original source data to a separate file.
  - From there, you would use a "working file" to slice, dice, and otherwise format your data.
  - When that's (finally) done, you're finally ready to the cleaned up and modified data for calculations.

- Reemphasizing concepts we covered earlier in this chapter, if you're relying solely on Excel when working with a large and complex dataset, what if there are changes to your source data (such as a change to the trial balance)?
  - The answer is that it's a _disaster_ that leaves you having to choose among unattractive alternatives.

- You can _rework your source data_ from scratch.
  - At best, this is monumentally boring, but you'll finally get there.
    - Oh, did I mention that before you finish, the source data will change again?
    - And did I also mention there is no guarantee that it won't change AGAIN after that?
  - Another problem in manually reworking large amounts of data is that it's prone to error.
    - Boredom doesn't pair well with the concentration needed to maintain accuracy.
    - That aside, you're human. Thus, even if you're making every effort to work carefully, the more data you're trying to manually manipulate, the greater the chance that you'll miss something.
    - These problems are compounded if you're working long hours to meet a deadline, such as publishing year-end financial statements or filing a tax return.

- As an alternative to entirely reworking your source data, you could try to narrow in on _only what changed_ in the source data from the prior version to the current version.
  - In theory, that sounds efficient, to only deal with what might just be a small out of data that changed.

- However, to do this, you first need a sufficient level of skill in Excel to pull it off.
- You also need to know the source data well enough to recognize changes when you seem them.
- Finally, even if you successfully narrow down your data to only what changed, you must be extremely when you "surgically insert" those changes into the Excel model containing your calculations.
  - Given how complex Excel models can be, and how many dependencies they can have built into them, such changes can easily blow up your calculation.

- In summary, anytime you make manual vs. automatic changes, you risk making errors and getting caught in a complex, time-consuming quagmire.

Summarizing the advantages of using Alteryx (vs. Excel) to dynamically manage your data

- By using Alteryx, you're managing your data according to a dynamic process, based on the layout and configuration of the tools in your workflow.

- This has some outrageously powerful implications. Summarizing this and other points we've covered previously, the advantages of using Alteryx to manage your data are as follows.

  1) You can hone the organization and format of your data within Alteryx, all while leaving your original source data untouched.

  2) You can see what's happening to your data as it passes through Alteryx, meaning that it's 100% traceable from the source to the output.

  3) You can set up Alteryx workflows to quickly adapt to and update changes in source data.
     a. From experience, I can say that it's not an exaggeration in many cases to be able to update data using Alteryx in 5-10 minutes.
     b. Who knows how long it will take to manually rework a large dataset using Excel on a standalone basis, but I can say from personal experience that it takes a _lot_ of work!

An on-the-job example to illustrate how Alteryx compliments and enhances Excel

- To illustrate these concepts with a real-world example, let's assume that I'm using Excel to do a complex tax calculation.
  - Because of all the twists and turns inherent in the tax rules, I find Excel to be the _perfect_ tool for the job.

- However, no matter how slick and sophisticated my Excel workbook may be, my tax calculation will *never* be correct unless it's based on accurate and up to date financial data from the general ledger ("GL").
  - With that in mind, I use the ERP system to extract what I need, which turns out to be 15,000 lines of data.
  - The good news is that I now have what I need to do my tax calculation, but that bad news is that I've got a large amount of data to deal with, and it's in a messy format.[17]

- Using principles and methods outlined in this book, I use Alteryx to clean up and organize the data and put it into the format that I need for my Excel calculations.
  - Once this is complete, I export the data to Excel using the "Output Data" tool.

- I copy the source data from the cleaned-up data file I created with Alteryx, and I paste it into the Excel workbook where I'm doing my tax calculations,
  - I put this source financial data (from Alteryx) in a separate tab labeled "GL Data."
  - From there, I build formulas throughout my Excel workbook that calculate figures that are derived from the GL source data.
  - Further, I link to and reference these figures throughout my Excel workbook as part of building out my tax calculation.
    - This means that all my tax calculations are based on the latest GL data, which is a *critical* aspect of creating an accurate work product.

- During this complex project, and under a tight deadline, I learn from the Accounting Group that there have been some "updates" to the GL.
  - This is "accounting-speak," a roundabout way of saying that they've booked additional entries to the GL.
  - Ahhhhhhh! This means the GL source data in my Excel file is now longer up to date, which means that all my tax calculations are off! ☹

- Taking a deep breath, I start the process of updating my Excel workbook by doing the following:

  1) I extract the updated GL data from the ERP system, and I save it to a new "unadjusted" (or raw) Excel file.
  2) I open my Alteryx workflow.
  3) I ensure that the "Input Data" tool is connected to the *updated*, raw GL data (from Step #1).
  4) I quickly re-check the Alteryx workflow to ensure that it still meets my needs.
     a. If the workflow worked like it was supposed to before, it should need few (if any) updates or modifications.

---

[17] So far, this kind of project should be sounding *extremely familiar* to accounting, tax, or finance professionals with any degree of experience!

b. As part of my checks, I make sure the name and filepath configured in the "Output Data" tool will save an updated (clean) Excel file with the name and to the location I want.

5) I re-run the workflow.

6) After that's done, I locate the clean and updated Excel file that was created by the Alteryx workflow (from Step #4b).

7) I copy the GL source data from the Alteryx-created Excel file, and I paste it into the "GL Data" tab in the Excel workbook where I'm doing my tax calculations.

8) Assuming I designed my Excel workbook correctly, the following will happen:

   a. All my figures based on GL data will _automatically update_ to their corrected amounts.

   b. These updated GL figures will flow to my tax-related computations, and they will automatically update as well.

- To finish off, what impact did using Alteryx to support my Excel computations have on my final work product?
  - I was able to spend significantly more time working through the complexities and nuances of the tax calculation.
    - This is the kind of work I was hired to do.
    - This is also the kind of work that I _enjoy_ doing.
  - I had more time to reference, document and support my work.
    - This is something that my reviewer found extremely helpful, and that reflected well on me.
    - This will also make a major positive difference when the calculation is audited (something that wasn't lost on my reviewer).
  - I was able to dramatically reduce the amount of time I spent organizing, formatting, and verifying source data.
    - Further, instead of considering working with data to be a pain, I found the process of building and customizing an Alteryx workflow to meet my needs to be interesting, engaging, and enjoyable.
  - I also increased the accuracy of my work product because:
    - I used a dynamic process to deal with the source data vs. a manual process that's more subject to human error.

- In summary, by using Alteryx to support my work in Excel, I was able to devote more time to the complexities of the tax calculation itself, which allowed more time for:
  - Checking and proving out my work.
  - Verifying that I applied the tax rules correctly and
  - Ensuring that my documentation for all of the above was clear, complete, concise, and logically organized.

9 Other Useful Data Cleansing and Formatting Tools

9.1 Learning Objectives

Upon the completion of this chapter, you will know how to use:

- "Input Data" to resolve delimited data formatting challenges.
- "Text to Columns" handle even more sophisticated delimited data formats.
- "Data Cleansing" to automatically clean up data formatting.
- "Select" to do date and time formatting.
- "DateTime" to handle even more sophisticated date and time formats.
- "Sort" to organize and reorder data.
- "Unique" to identify unique and duplicate data.

9.2 A Brief Review of Where We Are – "A Clean Block of Data"

The significance of what you can now do with Alteryx

- Before moving on, I think at this point it's worth pausing to consider where we are, as well as the significance of what we've covered so far. You're now able to:

    1) Import a massive amount of messy, disorganized data into Alteryx (the "Input Data" tool).
    2) Clean up the top section of the data ("Select Records").
    3) Automatically name all the columns in your data ("Dynamic Rename").
    4) Rename, reorder, and delete columns until you have them organized exactly the way that you want ("Select").
    5) You also know how to remove unnecessary rows that are cluttering up your data, as well as to pare it down to only those rows containing information that matters to you ("Filter").
    6) And finally, you know how to export your cleaned up data to an Excel file where you can use it to perform whatever calculations you want ("Output Data").
    7) In summary, you now know how to transform a large amount of disorganized data into "a clean block of data."

- Given that's true then, in baseball parlance, _you can now bring the heat!_

- "But wait!" you might protest. "I only know how to throw a few pitches using Alteryx! How can I possibly be effective?"
  - Just remember what I said earlier:

It's not how many pitches you can throw; it's how well you throw the pitches that you know.

- If you mastered only what we've covered so far, you're already light years ahead of where you were using only Excel in terms of data management.

- That's the good news, that you now have a solid base of Alteryx-related knowledge and skill to work from.
  - The *even better news* is that we're not going to stop there!
  - Strap in, because I'm now going to teach you Alteryx skills that will enable you to rocket forward, resolving even more sophisticated data-related challenges faced by accounting, tax, and finance professionals.

What's next

- In many cases, raw data is "clean enough" to be managed in a workflow using the tools and methods we've covered so far.

- However, there are times when these tools and techniques won't be enough, and you'll need some additional firepower to transform your data to meet your needs.

- With that in mind, the purpose of this chapter is to cover more advanced data cleaning tools and techniques.

9.3 How to Use the "Input Data" Tool to Handle Delimited Data

An introduction to delimited data and the traditional (Excel) method for dealing with it

- Delimited data is information (text, numbers, names, dates, etc.) that is set apart by a consistent separator such as a comma, space, tab, or pipe.

- Left in its delimited state, this kind of data gives Excel fits, because it can't automatically read the data (a sales figure) without the delimiter (a comma) causing interference.
  - By default, delimited data appears to Excel to run together as one continuous mass of information.

- The Excel method for dealing with delimited data is the "Text to Columns" tool that's located in the "Data" section of the ribbon.
  - Obviously, we're focused on Alteryx rather than Excel in this material.
  - Thus, to keep it short, I'll just say that in my experience the Excel approach to dealing with delimited data has been (very) hit and miss.
    - It rarely works cleanly for me and
    - It often leaves me with a fair amount of manual cleanup to do afterward.

- Admittedly, some of my problems may stem from the fact that I'm not using the Excel as skillfully and effectively as I could be.
  - However, given that Alteryx handles delimited data so easily and with such precision, it's my tool of choice for cleaning up and organizing data in non-standard formats.[18]

Recognizing delimited data formats is the first step

- Even if you use Alteryx (vs. Excel) to deal with delimited data, that doesn't automatically solve your problem.
  - To effectively work with delimited data, you must first _recognize it_ when you see it.

- In the subsections that follow, we'll review examples of common types of delimited data types, giving you the knowledge and understanding you need to spot them.

- In addition, we'll start with the easiest way to deal with delimited data, which is by using an Alteryx tool you're already familiar with – the "Input Data" tool.
  - From there, we'll go over the "Text to Columns" tool, which will enable you to handle even more sophisticated issues related to delimited data.

Comma delimited data

- Pictured is an example of a text (.txt) file containing delimited data.

- With the human eye, it's easy in this simple example to see what the data is telling you.
  - There are three columns – 1, 2 and 3.
  - Each of these columns has a progressively growing set of data.

```
Sample Data - Comma Delimited.txt

File   Edit   Format   View   Help

Col1,Col2,Col3
100,a1,b1
200,a2,b2
300,a3,b3
```

- You also notice that the data in each row is separated by commas.

---

[18] This goes back to the golf analogy that I shared earlier. Yes, I suppose I could use my Excel "putter" to hit delimited data off the tee. But I find that I have a lot more success dealing with delimited data when I use my Alteryx "driver" instead.

o That is the key to recognizing delimited data, to see that there is *a consistent pattern* that's separating the data.

- To import this data into Alteryx in a way the program can recognize how it's organized, we need to do the following.

    1) Drag an "Input Data" tool to the Canvas.
    2) Click on the "Input Data" tool to configure it.
    3) In the section, "Connect a File or Database," navigate to the text file containing the delimited data.
    4) After double-clicking on the text file, you'll see a pop-up window like the following.

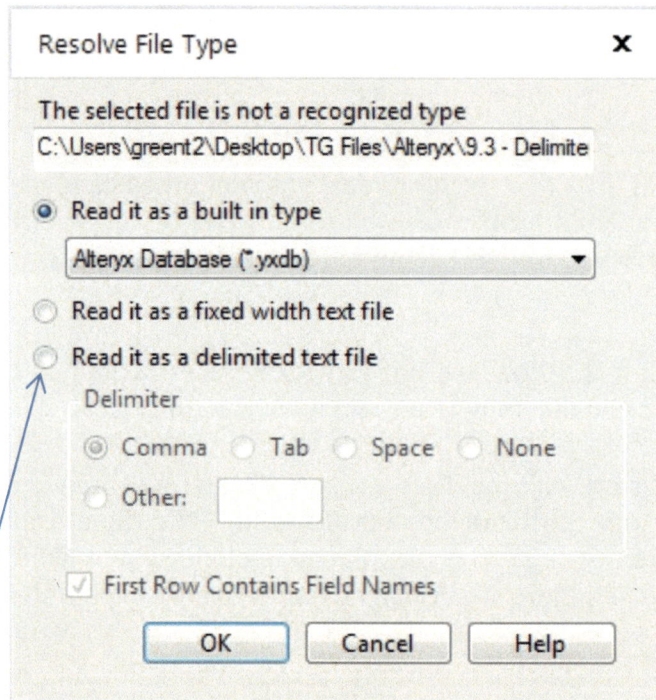

Input Data

Resolve File Type	✕

The selected file is not a recognized type
C:\Users\greent2\Desktop\TG Files\Alteryx\9.3 - Delimite

◉ Read it as a built in type

Alteryx Database (*.yxdb) ▼

◯ Read it as a fixed width text file

◯ Read it as a delimited text file

Delimiter

◉ Comma ◯ Tab ◯ Space ◯ None

◯ Other: [   ]

☑ First Row Contains Field Names

[OK] [Cancel] [Help]

5) Click the button "Read it (referring to your data) as a delimited text file."
6) Click "Comma" in the "Delimiter" section.
7) After you click "OK," you'll see the data organized the way we need it, as pictured to the right in the "Input Data" tool's preview pane.

	Col1	Col2	Col3
1	100	a1	b1
2	200	a2	b2
3	300	a3	b3

Tab delimited data

- Following is an example of tab delimited data.

```
Sample Data - Tab Delimited.txt - Notepad
File  Edit  Format  View  Help
TIMEKEEPER_NAME TIMEKEEPER_ID   BASE_RATE       EFFECTIVE_RATE  CURRENCY
POSTCODE        COUNTRY STATE_OR_PROVINCE       TIMEKEEPER_CLASSIFICATION
YOE     CLIENT_ID       LAW_FIRM_MATTER_ID      TIMEKEEPER_ETHNICITY
TIMEKEEPER_GENDER       TIMEKEEPER_LGBTQ        TIMEKEEPER_MILITARY_STATUS
TIMEKEEPER_DISABILITY
Timekeeper_1    13901   101.11  101.91  USD     98070   AFG             LA      1
                A       Male    Y       N       Y
Timekeeper_2    13902   102.21  102.81  USD     98071   ALB             AS      1
                P       Female  N       V       N
Timekeeper_3    13904   104.47  104.6   USD     98073   USA     AL      AS      1
                B       Male    Y       I       Y
```

- What a mess.
  - o Is there any possible way Alteryx can make sense of this?
  - o The answer is yes (and with incredible ease)!

- Follow the same steps as outlined in the subsection "Comma delimited data" above, except at Step 6 click the "Tab" (rather than the "Comma") button.

- After you click "OK," you will see the following in the "Input Data" tool's preview pane.

	TIMEKEEPER_NAME	TIMEKEEPER_ID	BASE_RATE	EFFECTIVE_RATE	CURRENCY	POSTC(
1	Timekeeper_1	13901	101.11	101.91	USD	98070
2	Timekeeper_2	13902	102.21	102.81	USD	98071
3	Timekeeper_3	13904	104.47	104.6	USD	98073

- Pretty incredible, yes?
  - o As I've said before, by having to spend less time fighting with data, you'll have more time to focus on the interesting and engaging aspects of your work.

Pipe delimited data

- Following is an example of pipe delimited data.
  - o A "pipe," by the way, is this symbol: |

```
Sample Data - Pipe Dlimited.txt - Notepad
File  Edit  Format  View  Help
TIMEKEEPER_NAME|TIMEKEEPER_ID|BASE_RATE|EFFECTIVE_RATE|CURRENCY|POSTCODE|COUNTRY|
STATE_OR_PROVINCE|TIMEKEEPER_CLASSIFICATION|YOE|CLIENT_ID|LAW_FIRM_MATTER_ID|
TIMEKEEPER_ETHNICITY|TIMEKEEPER_GENDER|TIMEKEEPER_LGBTQ|
TIMEKEEPER_MILITARY_STATUS|TIMEKEEPER_DISABILITY
Timekeeper_1|13901|101.11|101.91|USD|98070| |AFG|LA|1| | |A|Male|Y|N|Y
Timekeeper_2|13902|102.21|102.81|USD|98071| |ALB|AS|1| | |P|Female|N|V|N
Timekeeper_3|13904|104.47|104.6|USD|98073|USA|AL|AS|1| | |B|Male|Y|I|Y
```

- Similar to how you handled the tab delimiters, follow the steps outlined previously until you get to Step 6.

- o Here, however, you will notice that there is no "Pipe" option to click.
- o Instead, click "Other" and then put a pipe (|) in the blank field.

  ⦿ Read it as a delimited text file

  Delimiter

  ○ Comma ○ Tab ○ Space ○ None

  ⦿ Other: | |

- o After you click "OK," you will see the illustration that follows in the "Input Data" tool's preview pane.

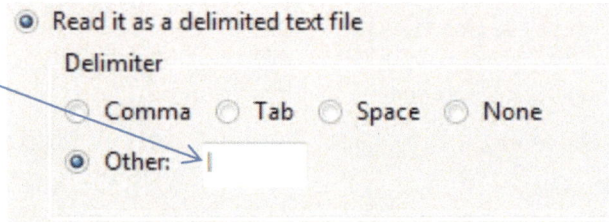

	TIMEKEEPER_NAME	TIMEKEEPER_ID	BASE_RATE	EFFECTIVE_RATE	CURRENCY	POSTCODE
1	Timekeeper_1	13901	101.11	101.91	USD	98070
2	Timekeeper_2	13902	102.21	102.81	USD	98071
3	Timekeeper_3	13904	104.47	104.6	USD	98073

- An important thing to recognize here is that the "Other" field not only gives you the ability handle pipe delimited data, but also the flexibility to deal with other non-standard delimiters such as:
  - o Apostrophes
  - o Dashes, etc.

9.4 Use the "Text to Columns" Tool to Handle Special Delimited Data Challenges

Keep it simple...until you can't

- As I've said time and again, I'm a HUGE believer in keeping things simple to the extent possible.

- As it relates to Alteryx, that means using the "fastball" tools as your disposal before rushing off to learn more obscure, specialized tools (the "curveballs").
  - o There are times, however, when the tools currently in your toolbox simply won't do, and you need a new one to tackle a specific job.

- In the previous section, we saw how well the "Input Data" tool handled delimited data.
  - o While the datasets in those examples were small, the same methods can be successfully applied to *massive* datasets.
  - o In the example below, however, we've got a problem that's too much for the "Input Data" tool to handle.

The problem of delimited data in a single column

	Transaction_date	Product	Price	Payment_Type	Name	Location
1	2009-01-02 06:17:00	Product1	1200	Mastercard	carolina	Basildon, England, United Kingdom
2	2009-01-02 04:53:00	Product1	1200	Visa	Betina	Parkville, MO, United States
3	2009-01-02 13:08:00	Product1	1200	Mastercard	Federica e Andrea	Astoria, OR, United States
4	2009-01-03 14:44:00	Product1	1200	Visa	Gouya	Echuca, Victoria, Australia
5	2009-01-04 12:56:00	Product2	3600	Visa	Gerd W	Cahaba Heights, AL, United States

- In our previous sales datasets, city, state or territory, and country data was conveniently broken out in separate columns.
    - However, in the example above, all the location data is "mashed together" in a single column (the "Location" field – see the illustration above).

- In its present state, this format is going to wreak havoc on our Excel analysis. This is important because:
    - We need sales broken down by city for sales tax purposes.
    - We need sales broken down by state for income tax purposes.
    - We need sales broken down by country for regional management purposes, and this is also a key metric followed by analysts on Wall Street.

- In summary, we <u>MUST</u> break our sales data down by city, state or territory, and country.

An example of using the "Text to Columns" tool to parse data in columns

- How can this be done? The first step is to recognize that the data in the "Location" field (or column) is separated by commas.
    - In Alteryx terms, when data in a column is <u>*consistently*</u> separated with the <u>*same character*</u> then it is delimited.
        - Said another way to be clear, the data in the "Location" column is delimited by commas.

- When data is delimited, Alteryx tools can be used to "parse" it, meaning to break it into the separate pieces that we need.
    - Specifically, we'll use the "Text to Columns" tool to parse the data in the "Location" field (or column).

Text To Columns

- To accomplish this, follow these steps.

1) If it's not already in your Favorites section, click on the "Parse" section of the Tool Palette, find the "Text to Columns" tool, and drag it to the Canvas.
    a. In this case, we're placing the "Text to Columns" tool beside "Dynamic Rename," because the data coming out of the former tool's output anchor contains the "Location" column that we want to parse.

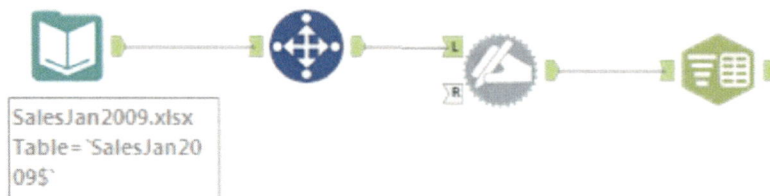

SalesJan2009.xlsx
Table= `SalesJan20
09$`

2) Click on the "Text to Columns" tool to configure it.

Select Column to Split

Column to split   Delimiters

Location

⦿ Split to columns

Number of columns   3

Extra characters   Leave extra in last column

Output root name   New Location

3) In the "Column to split" section, use the down arrow to select the "Location" column.
4) In the "Delimiters" section, type a comma.

5) Type "3" in the "Number of columns" section, because we want the "Location" column to be split into three different columns.
    a. One for city, one for state/territory, and one for country.
    b. If you encounter a situation where you're not sure how many columns you need, it's better to overestimate because it's easier to see and correct in the output.

6) In the "Output root name" type "New Location."
    a. See the comments following the next illustration to see what this does.

7) Run the workflow.
    a. (As an optional step, I also used the "Select" tool to remove all but location-related data in the output that follows).

Location	New Location1	New Location2	New Location3
1 Basildon, England, United Kingdom	Basildon	England	United Kingdom
2 Parkville, MO, United States	Parkville	MO	United States
3 Astoria, OR, United States	Astoria	OR	United States
4 Echuca, Victoria, Australia	Echuca	Victoria	Australia
5 Cahaba Heights, AL, United States	Cahaba Heights	AL	United States

- Note how the "Text to Columns" tool did NOT impact the data in the original "Location" column.
    - This is a major improvement over the Excel "Text to Columns" approach, which DOES alter the data in the column to which it's applied.

- Instead, Designer created three new fields (or columns) based on the "New Location" description we typed in as the "Output root name" in Step 6.
    - Recall in Step 5 that we configured the tool to split the "Location" column into three columns.
    - This is what's creating the column names New Location1, New Location2 and NewLocation3.

- As a final cleanup (not illustrated above), we could place a "Select" tool after "Text to Columns" to rename the "New Location 1-2-3" columns as:
    - City
    - State or Territory and
    - Country.

What happens if you configure the tool to "Split to rows?"

- What happens if you configure the tool to "Split to rows" of the "Location" column?

Column to split	Delimiters
Location	⌄	,

◯ Split to columns

⦿ Split to rows

- The output illustrated below shows what happened each time the tool encountered a delimiter (a comma in this example) in the "Location" column.
    - A new line of data was created.
    - The new line of data was the same as the previous one EXCEPT
    - Locations were progressively broken out (city, state, territory) until Designer came to the next record (another location), and the process repeated.

	Transaction_date	Product	Price	Payment_Type	Name	Location
1	2009-01-02 06:17:00	Product1	1200	Mastercard	carolina	Basildon
2	2009-01-02 06:17:00	Product1	1200	Mastercard	carolina	England
3	2009-01-02 06:17:00	Product1	1200	Mastercard	carolina	United Kingdom
4	2009-01-02 04:53:00	Product1	1200	Visa	Betina	Parkville
5	2009-01-02 04:53:00	Product1	1200	Visa	Betina	MO
6	2009-01-02 04:53:00	Product1	1200	Visa	Betina	United States

- As you can see, this output is somewhat confusing. As a result, you will use the "Split to columns" setting most of the time.

Other things to keep in mind when configuring the "Text to Columns" tool

- The "Text to Columns" tool can only be used to parse columns that are categorized as strings (or text).
  - o Thus, this tool will work on a column that's coded with a "V_String" data type.
  - o If you want to parse a column that's categorized as a number or a date, you'll first have to use a "Select" tool to code the column data type as a "V_String."

- The "Text to Columns" tool can only be used to parse ONE column at a time.
  - o However, there is nothing stopping you from using one "Text to Columns" tool after another.
  - o This convention, of using the same tool in a progressive fashion, is often employed in workflows for a number of reasons.[19]

9.5 How the "Data Cleansing" Tool Improves Your Data

What is data cleansing and why is it important?

- Before we declare victory and export the data from the "Text to Columns" example straight to Excel, we should take a closer look.

- Notice that three of the four columns in the illustration that follows are underlined in red, and more than half of the visible cells are flagged with a red tick mark.
  - o What does that mean (remember, it's in red, so it can't be good ☹)?

	Location	New Location1	New Location2	New Location3
1	Basildon, England, United Kingdom	Basildon	England	United Kingdom
2	Parkville, MO, United States	Parkville	MO	United States
3	Astoria, OR, United States	Astoria	OR	United States
4	Echuca, Victoria, Australia	Echuca	Victoria	Australia
5	Cahaba Heights, AL, United States	Cahaba Heights	AL	United States

---

[19] We saw an example of this with the "Filter" tool on page 87.

- Designer underlines columns in red if it detects potential problems or inconsistencies in the data.
  - In this case, if you place your cursor over the red tick mark by "United Kingdom," you see the following warning message:
    - "This cell has leading spaces."
  - If you place your cursor over the red tick mark by "United States" the problem is even worse:
    - "This cell has leading and trailing spaces."

- Data with leading and trailing spaces can cause problems if it's exported to Excel.

- For example, if leading spaces exist, Excel does not see:
  - "United Kingdom"
  - Instead, Excel sees: "[space, space, space] United Kingdom."
  - These kinds of spaces can create problems in Excel with:
    - Sorting
    - Formula references
    - VLOOKUPS, and so on.

Using the "Data Cleansing" tool to clear leading and trailing white spaces

- Rather than slog through Excel fixing the kinds of issues described above, you can quickly and efficiently use the "Data Cleansing" tool while you're still working with your data in Alteryx.

- In our example, we noticed the problems with our data (the red marks and underlines) when we clicked on the output anchor of the "Select" tool.
  - As a result, we'll place a "Data Cleansing" tool after the "Select" tool but before the "Output Data" tool (as shown below).

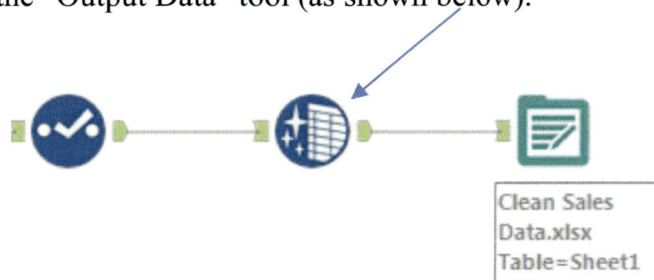

- Click on the "Date Cleansing" tool to configure it.

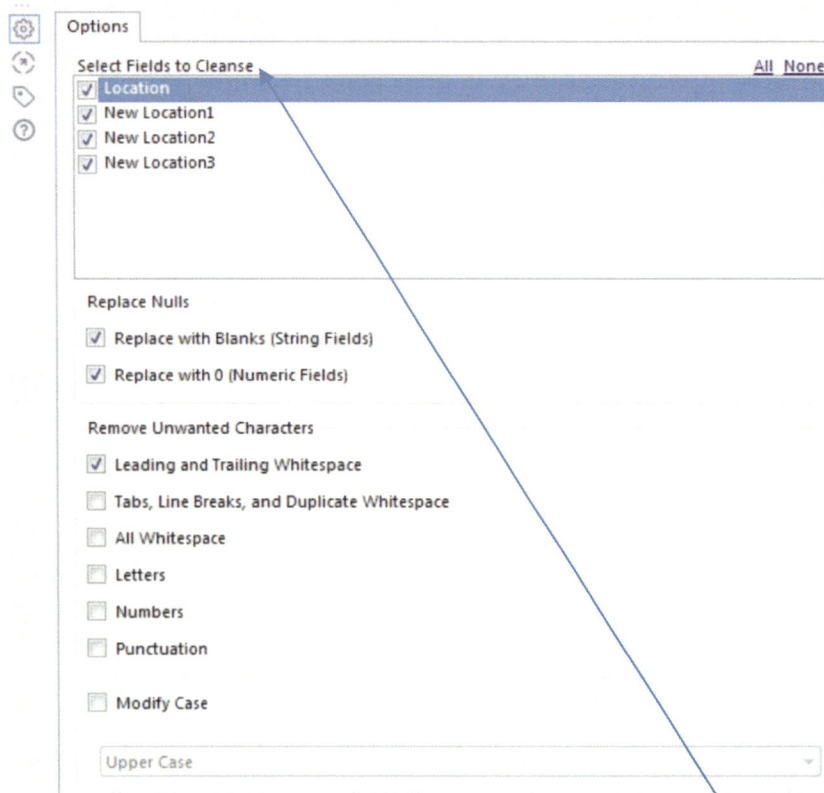

- By default, all active fields (or columns) will be checked in the section "Select Fields to Cleanse."
  - If this doesn't happen, you can click on "All" in the top right of the configuration to check them all at once.

- In the "Remove Unwanted Characters" section, be sure to click:
  - "Leading and Trailing Whitespace."
  - While the "Replace Null" boxes were also checked by default, that has no impact on our dataset since it contained no null values.

- After running the workflow, all problems that were flagged in red will be cleared (nothing is marked in red in the illustration below!).

	Location	New Location1	New Location2	New Location3
1	Basildon, England, United Kingdom	Basildon	England	United Kingdom
2	Parkville, MO, United States	Parkville	MO	United States
3	Astoria, OR, United States	Astoria	OR	United States
4	Echuca, Victoria, Australia	Echuca	Victoria	Australia
5	Cahaba Heights, AL, United States	Cahaba Heights	AL	United States

Other uses of the "Data Cleansing" tool

- In addition to clearing white space, the "Data Cleansing" tool has other uses.

- As previously noted, it can manage how null values are displayed.
  - You can choose to make nulls blank or replace them with zeros.

- You can also remove unwanted characters from your data.
  - When you select this, ALL of what you choose is removed.
  - For example, if you check "Punctuation" as a configuration option, ALL punctuation will be removed from ALL your data.

- Finally, you can use the "Data Cleansing" tool to modify the case of your data:
  - Upper Case – This changes all characters in a column to upper case.
  - Lower Case – This changes all characters to lower case.
  - Title Case – This automatically capitalizes the first letter of each word.

Using the "Data Cleansing" tool vs. Alteryx "functions" to clean data

- As the basis for making a point, in Excel I can sum a column of numbers in one of two ways.

- The "manual" way is as follows:
  - I click on a cell.
  - I press the equal ("=") key.
  - From memory, I type "sum."
  - I click on the open parenthesis.
  - I use my mouse to select the cells I want to sum.
  - I click on the close parenthesis key.
  - After clicking "Enter," the sum formula executes and returns the value.
  - Okay…I'm exhausted. ☺

- A much easier way to accomplish the same thing in Excel is to click on the "AutoSum" button, click Enter, and you're done.

  Σ AutoSum ▾

- This example illustrates a practice that I employ when using Excel.
  - Namely, I don't waste time and effort memorizing steps when there's a function or button (such as the "AutoSum" button) that's pre-built to do the job.

- How does this apply to the "Data Cleansing" tool?

- As you may have noticed, the "Data Cleansing" tool has some limitations.
  - For example, removing ALL letters from data? That's a bit of a blunt tool.
  - Similarly, the "Modify Case" options don't address all capitalization-related scenarios you might encounter.

- However, despite these shortcomings, the "Data Cleaning" tool is powerful for this reason:
  - It enables you to use a TOOL to do all that's necessary in many cases to clean up your data.

- Alternatively, if you skip past the "Data Cleansing" tool to scrub your data, then you're faced with:
  - Using what Alteryx refers to as "Functions" (such as "Trim") within the "Formula" tool.
  - Using the "RegEx" tool.
  - These are both far more advanced methods of cleaning up data, and both are beyond the scope of this book.

- In summary, despite its limitations, the "Data Cleansing" tool is extremely useful because it provides you with an easy and intuitive way to resolve *many* data-related clean-up issues without having to resort to more complicated methods for doing do.

9.6   How to Use the "Select" Tool to Handle Dates

- Recall from our discussion of data types[20] that dates are entirely from numeric ("Double") and text ("V_String") data.

- Referring to our sales example, the "Transaction Date" field (or column) is currently coded in the "Select" tool as a "V_String" data type.

Field	Type	Size	Rename
☑ Transaction_date	V_String ▾	255	Transaction Date

- As a result, while the output showing in the Results Window for the "Transaction Date" column LOOKS like a date and time, Designer is treating it (or reading it) as nothing more than text.

- If, instead, you want Alteryx to display AND process the data in the "Transaction Date" column as a date, you need to select "Date" as the data type, as show in the illustration that follows.

Field	Type	Size	Rename
☑ Transaction_date	Date ▾	10	Transaction Date

---

[20] See page 72.

- After doing so, upon re-running the workflow, your output will display as shown to the right in the Results Window.

	Transaction Date
1	2009-01-02
2	2009-01-02
3	2009-01-02
4	2009-01-03
5	2009-01-04

- Remember, this is about more than just appearances.
  - By selecting "Date" for the "Transaction Date" field, both Excel and Alteryx will be able to perform time-related calculations with that data.

- As a final example, here is what happens to the output when we choose each of the following time-related data types (illustrated below):
  - Transaction Date – "Date" displays the date only.
  - Last Login – "Time" displays the time of day only.
  - Date Account Created – "DateTime" displays the date and time.

	Transaction Date	Last Login	Date Account Created
1	2009-01-02	06:08:00	2009-01-02 06:00:00
2	2009-01-02	07:49:00	2009-01-02 04:42:00
3	2009-01-02	12:32:00	2009-01-01 16:21:00
4	2009-01-03	14:22:00	2005-09-25 21:13:00
5	2009-01-04	12:45:00	2008-11-15 15:47:00

9.7 Use the "DateTime" Tool for Advanced Time and Date Formatting

DateTime

The primary purposes of the "DateTime" tool

- The "DateTime" is used primarily for two things.

  1) To convert text (or "string") and other data types to *date* data types.
     - As we just reviewed, in most instances, this can be easily handled using the "Select" tool.

  2) To convert dates in one date format (2020-06-30) to another date format (June 30, 2020).

- Again, because the "Select" tool can accomplish Item #1, we'll turn our attention to Item #2.

Converting date formats

- As a reminder, following is the date-related output that was displayed from our sales data.

	Transaction Date	Last Login	Date Account Created
1	2009-01-02	06:08:00	2009-01-02 06:00:00
2	2009-01-02	07:49:00	2009-01-02 04:42:00
3	2009-01-02	12:32:00	2009-01-01 16:21:00
4	2009-01-03	14:22:00	2005-09-25 21:13:00
5	2009-01-04	12:45:00	2008-11-15 15:47:00

- Let's assume that for presentational and reporting purposes, the "Transactional Date" column needs to be in the format "January 1, 2009." [21]

- To accomplish this, locate the "DateTime" tool in the "Parse" section of the Tool Palette, drag it to the Canvas, and place it after the tool that contains the data you want to convert.
  - In this case, we're placing it after the "Select" tool, because that's what's outputting the date-related data shown in the previous illustration.
  - Click the star by the "DateTime" tool in the Tool Palette if you want to add it to the "Favorites" section.

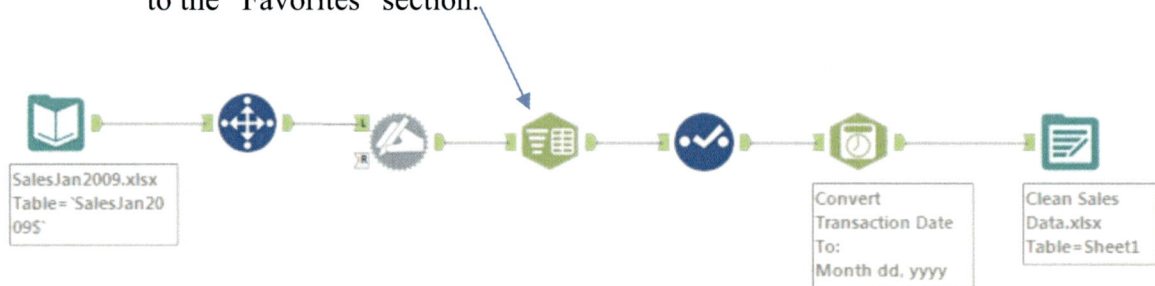

SalesJan2009.xlsx
Table=`SalesJan2009$`

Convert
Transaction Date
To:
Month dd, yyyy

Clean Sales
Data.xlsx
Table=Sheet1

- Now click on the "DateTime" tool and configure it as follows.

[This space was intentionally left blank].

---

[21] If you haven't noticed by now, all the sales data in the examples in this book date back to 2009. It just happened to be a dataset that I liked to illustrate numerous examples, but I should have updated the year!

- Note the following.
  - We need to select the option "Date/Time format to a string."
    - This is because we previously used the "Select" tool to choose a "Date" data type for the "Transaction Date" column.
  - Choose "Transaction Date" for the option "Select the date/time field to convert."
  - For "Specify the new column name:"
    - "DateTime_Out" is the default.
    - Instead, we have typed in "New Transaction Date" as the name of the column that will contain our updated date formatting.
  - In the section "Select the format for the new column," look for the date pattern that aligns with what you want.
    - We select "Month dd, yyyy."
      - "Month" spelled out means the full name of the month will display in the output.
  - When we re-run the workflow, our output produces the following.

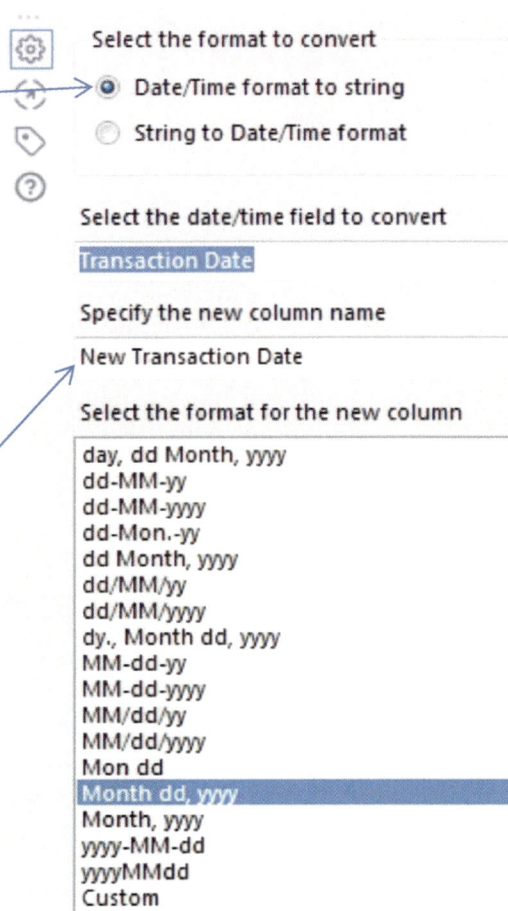

	Transaction Date	Last Login	Date Account Created	New Transaction Date
1	2009-01-02	06:08:00	2009-01-02 06:00:00	January 02, 2009
2	2009-01-02	07:49:00	2009-01-02 04:42:00	January 02, 2009
3	2009-01-02	12:32:00	2009-01-01 16:21:00	January 02, 2009
4	2009-01-03	14:22:00	2005-09-25 21:13:00	January 03, 2009
5	2009-01-04	12:45:00	2008-11-15 15:47:00	January 04, 2009

- Note that the "DateTime" tool did not delete or otherwise modify the original "Transaction Date" column.
  - Instead, the tool created an additional column with the label we chose above – "New Transaction Date."

Select the format to convert
- ◉ Date/Time format to string
- ○ String to Date/Time format

Select the date/time field to convert
Transaction Date

Specify the new column name
New Transaction Date

Select the format for the new column
day, dd Month, yyyy
dd-MM-yy
dd-MM-yyyy
dd-Mon.-yy
dd Month, yyyy
dd/MM/yy
dd/MM/yyyy
dy., Month dd, yyyy
MM-dd-yy
MM-dd-yyyy
MM/dd/yy
MM/dd/yyyy
Mon dd
Month dd, yyyy
Month, yyyy
yyyy-MM-dd
yyyyMMdd
Custom

9.8   Organize Your Data Using "Sort"

In general

- The "Sort" tool allows you to visually order your data in whatever way works best for organization, interpretation, or analysis.

- To be clear, I have no complaints with Excel's sort feature; I don't ever recall having and significant problems or struggles with it.

- That said, if you know in advance that you need your data sorted prior to using it for Excel calculations, it's extremely fast and convenient to do it as part of an Alteryx workflow.

An example of using the "Sort" tool

- Let's assume that our sales data is currently organized as follows.

	Transaction Date	Product	Sales Price	Credit Card	Country
1	2009-01-02	Product1	1200	Mastercard	United Kingdom
2	2009-01-02	Product1	1200	Visa	United States
3	2009-01-02	Product1	1200	Mastercard	United States
4	2009-01-03	Product1	1200	Visa	Australia
5	2009-01-04	Product2	3600	Visa	United States

- The data is currently sorted by "Transaction Date" in ascending order (or starting at the earliest point in time).

- For our Excel analysis, assume it would be more helpful to have our output sorted by credit card, then by country and lastly by date.
    - To accomplish this, after dragging the "Sort" tool to the Canvas and connecting it to our workflow, we would configure it as follows.

☑ Use Dictionary Order   English (United States)

Fields

Name	Order
Credit Card	Ascending
Country	Ascending
Transaction Date	Ascending

- After doing so, our output will be sorted to like this:
  - Credit card followed by
  - Country followed by
  - Transaction date.

	Transaction Date	Product	Sales Price	Credit Card	Country
1	2009-01-02	Product1	1200	Mastercard	United Kingdom
2	2009-01-02	Product1	1200	Mastercard	United States
3	2009-01-03	Product1	1200	Visa	Australia
4	2009-01-02	Product1	1200	Visa	United States
5	2009-01-04	Product2	3600	Visa	United States

Fine tuning the "Sort" tool settings

- The sorts in the configuration tool will be applied to your data in order, starting at the top and working down.

- For string (text) data, you will generally sort in ascending order.
  - Ascending order is A, B, C, etc.
  - By default, sorting is done by ASCII characters.
    - This means a comma at the beginning of a word will be sorted at the top.
    - Capitalization can also throw the ordering off what you might expect.
  - If you're encountering these kinds of issues, you can fix them by checking "Use Dictionary Order" in the "Configuration" section.
    - In making this selection, Alyeryx looks past things such as ASCII formatting when sorting data.

☑ Use Dictionary Order | English (United States) |

- For numbers, ascending order is 1, 2, 3, etc.

- For dates, ascending order is older (January 1, 2000) to newer (December 31, 2000).

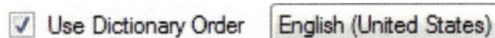

9.9 The "Unique" Tool Identifies Unique Data _and_ Duplicate Entries

The common need to identify duplicates within data

- It's _very_ common for accounting, tax, and finance professionals to want to confirm whether there are duplicates in a dataset.
  - In many datasets there shouldn't be ANY duplicates, so testing for them is a way to verify the integrity of the data.

- Consistent with the previous point, testing for duplicates is a way to avoid double-counting, something that can destroy the accuracy of your calculations.

- There are a couple of ways to find duplicates in Excel.

  1) Sorting – With a smaller dataset you can sort data.
     - From there you scan through it, looking for rows that contain the exact same data.
     - This ad hoc "scanning method" works fine for a smaller dataset, but quickly becomes tedious and prone to human error for larger ones.

  2) Conditional Formatting – A faster and more reliable way to detect duplicates is to use Excel's "Conditional Formatting" tool located in the "Home" section of the Ribbon.
     - In the section "Highlight Cell Rules," you can choose "Duplicate Values."
     - This will cause any duplicate entries in the column you select to be highlighted in a pinkish red, making them easier to identify.
     - This method involves some steps, but it's still a solidly good way to detect duplicates, even in datasets that contain a few thousand lines.
     - Note that while Excel makes it relatively easy to _detect_ duplicates, _removing_ them is trickier.
     - Using Alteryx to detect and remove duplicates is quicker, cleaner, and more intuitive that doing it in Excel.

An example of using the "Unique" tool to quickly identify duplicate data

- Returning to our sales analysis example, let's assume that each individual sale is assigned a unique transaction number.

- Knowing this, one of the procedures you want to employ to confirm the integrity of your data is to test for duplicate sales transactions.

- To do this using Alteryx, locate the "Unique" tool in the "Preparation" section of the "Tool Palette" and drag it to the workflow.
  - In this case, we're placing the tool to the right of the "Data Cleansing" tool, because its output contains the cleaned-up sales data that we want to test for duplicates.

- Click on the "Unique" tool and configure it as follows:
  - Click the box for the "Transaction #" column.
  - Since every sales transaction is assigned a unique number, this selection is all that's needed to surface any duplicates.

Column names

☐ Transaction Date

☑ Transaction #

☐ Product

☐ Sales Price

- From workflow illustration on the previous page, notice that the "Unique" tool has two output anchors.
  - The "U" output anchor contains all lines from the dataset that are unique.
  - The "D" output anchor separates out transactions that contain a duplicate transaction number.

- After running the workflow, when we click on the "D" output anchor we'll see the following.

Transaction Date	Transaction #	Product	Sales Price	Credit Card	Country
1 2009-01-11 04:29:00	25964627	Product3	7500	Visa	United States
2 2009-01-11 02:04:00	38298757	Product1	1200	Visa	Australia

- To be clear, the "D" output anchor only displays lines that were DUPLICATED in the data.
  - Said another way, these same sales transactions are STILL in our main dataset, but now they are only listed ONCE and not twice because the "Unique" tool has removed the duplicate entries.

- When we click on the "U" output anchor we see the following.

Transaction Date	Transaction #	Product	Sales Price	Credit Card	Country
1 2009-01-01 20:21:00	10003441	Product1	1200	Visa	United States
2 2009-01-18 11:03:00	10062758	Product2	3600	Amex	Spain
3 2009-01-25 15:18:00	10068057	Product2	3600	Visa	United States
4 2009-01-04 13:17:00	10289558	Product1	1200	Mastercard	Israel
5 2009-01-26 08:00:00	10323237	Product1	1200	Amex	United States
6 2009-01-07 00:12:00	10484944	Product2	3600	Mastercard	Switzerland
7 2009-01-13 18:08:00	10663416	Product1	1200	Amex	United States

- Again, this dataset contains our cleaned-up sales transactions, and knowing that it contains no duplicates will enable us to perform our Excel calculations with greater speed, accuracy, and confidence.

10 Using the "Join" and "Union" Tools to Combine Datasets

10.1 Learning Objectives

Upon the completion of this chapter, you will:

- Know the purpose and significance of the "Join" tool.
- Be able to use the "Join" tool to:
  - "Blend" data from two different datasets.
  - Identify similarities and differences between datasets.
- Recognize why it's better to use the "Select" rather than the "Join" tool to manage columns in data.
- Know the purpose and significance of the "Union" tool, and how its "stacking" of data differs from the "Join" tool's "blending" of data.
- Know how to use the "Union" tool to combine uniform datasets.
- Learn more advanced "Union" tool strategies and configuration techniques for combining non-uniform datasets.
- Recognize how combining the use of the "Join" and "Union" tools in the same workflow contributes to more complete and enhanced output, learn the methods within Alteryx for doing so.
- Be able to understand and explain why Alteryx is so much faster and more efficient at combining data than doing so manually using Excel.

10.2 The Significance and Purposes of the "Join" Tool

Transitioning from working with single to multiple sets of data

- To this point, you have steadily increased your knowledge and skill in working with a SINGLE set of data.

- In this chapter, we'll cover the use of Alteryx tools, methods and techniques that will enable you to combine MULTIPLE datasets efficiently and accurately.

- The first method we'll cover for combining datasets is using the "Join" tool.[22]

---

[22] Based on my observations and experience, the "Join" tool is part of the solution to *many* accounting, tax and finance data-related goals, challenges and objectives.

10.3 Use the "Join" Tool to Blend and Evaluate Data from Different Sources

An example of the usefulness of combining data

- It's extremely useful for accounting, tax, and finance professionals to be able to "blend" data from two different datasets.

- To illustrate what this means, let's say that you have a role that involves US-based entities, and you have access to a database that looks like this.

Entity Number	EIN	State	Headcount	Total Assets	Functional Currency
E0010	12-3456789	DE	1	100	USD
E0050	00-0005555	KS	282	7,000,000	USD
E0100	10-1111000	NY	60	1,500,000	USD
E0200	22-2222222	CA	74	1,800,000	USD
E0300	33-3333333	TX	804	20,000,000	USD
E0700	77-7777777	NC	27	750,000	USD
E0800	88-8888888	FL	83	2,075,000	USD
E0900	99-9999999	WA	162	4,050,000	USD
E1100	11-1111111	GA	325	8,575,000	USD

- This information is helpful – even vital – in your day-to-day work.
  - However, this dataset is not without (serious) shortcomings.
  - As one example, it doesn't contain entity names (only entity numbers).
  - This, and other missing data, causes you to have to go through multiple manual processes to fill in the gaps as you perform calculations and produce reports.[23]

[This space was intentionally left blank].

---

[23] Is it entirely realistic that your primary dataset would be this sparse? No, of course not. My goal here less about being perfectly realistic, and more about setting up an example to clearly illustrate the use and benefits of the "Join" tool.

- Let's now assume that you have a meeting with a team that deals with all entities (US and international). As part of your discussions, you discover that they have access to an entity database that contains the information that follows.

Entity #	Entity Name	Functional Currency	Country	Office Location	Contact	Total Sales
E0050	Fifty	USD	United States	Kansas City	Andy	19,740,000
E0100	One Hundred	USD	United States	New York	Bill	4,200,000
E0200	Two Hundred	USD	United States	Los Angelas	Martha	5,180,000
E0300	Three Hundred	USD	United States	Houston	Nancy	56,280,000
E0400	Four Hundred	EUR	Switzerland	Bern	Max	27,580,000
E0500	Five Hundred	JPY	Japan	Tokyo	Hichi	37,600,000
E0600	Six Hundred	USD	Germany	Berlin	Wally	8,200,000
E0700	Seven Hundred	USD	United States	Raleigh	Tony	1,890,000
E0800	Eight Hundred	USD	United States	Miami	Michael	5,810,000
E0900	Nine Hundred	USD	United States	Seattle	Aaron	11,340,000
E1000	One Thousand	EUR	France	Paris	Simone	16,900,000
E1100	Eleven Hundred	USD	United States	Atlanta	Barbara	19,740,000
E1200	Twelve Hundred	GBP	United Kingdom	London	Kurt	34,300,000

- You immediately recognize that it would be extremely useful for you (and others in your organization) to combine the information in your U.S. company database and the one pictured above, but there are some challenges.
    - You're extremely busy, and you don't have much time for another side project (yes, you're unique that way ☺).
    - Only a few sample lines are shown from each database.
        - In reality, you're part of a large and complex organization, and each database actually contains hundreds of lines of detail.
        - Combining such a large amount of data using Excel by itself would be a tedious and time-consuming exercise!

- Again, while you believe there would be tremendous value in combining the datasets for current and future projects, you're under enough "get-things-done-now" performance-related pressure that you feel like you've only got two options.
    - You can toss the idea datasets into the massive junk bin at your organization labeled, "High Value-Added Projects to be Completed 'One Day' When There Is Time."
    - You use some of your limited time to quickly and accurately combine the datasets using Alteryx's "Join" tool.

- Since you're not willing to walk away from a challenge and leave so much benefit on the table, we'll now focus on the *second* approach!

Identify your primary and secondary datasets in preparation for using the "Join" tool

- In preparing to use the "Join" tool, it's important clearly identify what I will refer to as your "primary" dataset and your "secondary" dataset.

- Think of your primary dataset is your "base" data.
  - In other words, this is what you use as your core data in Excel and other software applications.
  - Your intention is to use the "Join" tool to improve your core data by adding more information to it.

- The secondary dataset contains data and information that you want extract and _blend into_ your primary dataset.
  - Said another way, your intention is NOT to add to or update the secondary dataset.
  - You essentially want to pull data from it, add it to your primary dataset and then "walk away."[24]

- In our example:
  - You designate the U.S. entity database (in an Excel file named "Entity Data 1") as your primary dataset since it's the one that you regularly work with, and the one you want to improve for your day-to-day work.
  - The global database is in an Excel file named "Entity Data 2."
    - You view this as your secondary dataset since it contains data you want to pull from to add to and improve your primary dataset.

- Having identified your primary and secondary datasets, the next step is to use "Input Data" tools to bring them into Alteryx.
  - As shown in the illustration to the right, it's a good practice to position the primary dataset ("Entity Data 1") above the secondary dataset ("Entity Data 2").
  - This step also introduces a new and powerful concept alluded to at the beginning of the chapter – that you can import _multiple_ datasets into an Alteryx workflow.
    - Further, you're not limited to just two; you can import as many datasets into a workflow as you need to accomplish your goals.

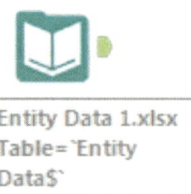

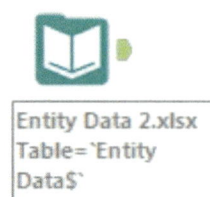

Entity Data 1.xlsx
Table=`Entity
Data$`

Entity Data 2.xlsx
Table=`Entity
Data$`

---

[24] This is a bit simplistic since you may have a need or desire to make improvements to the secondary dataset as well. However, to keep our example clean, we'll set aside that consideration for now.

How to use the "Join by Specific Fields" option to combine entity datasets

- With our primary and secondary datasets now on the Canvas the beginning of our workflow, we're ready to blend the second into the first by using the "Join" tool.
    - o This brings up an important point, which is that the "Join" tool can only be used to blend TWO datasets at a time.

- Drag a "Join" tool to the workflow and place it to the right of the "Input Data" tools.
    - o If it doesn't happen automatically, connect the primary dataset ("Entity Data 1") to the "Join" tool.
        - To do this, click on the output anchor of "Entity Data 1" and continue holding down the mouse button.
        - Move your cursor to the "L" (or "Left") input anchor of the "Join" tool.
        - When you let go of the mouse button, the output anchor of "Entity Data 1" should be connected to the "L" input anchor of the "Join" tool with a solid black line (as pictured).
    - o Follow the same process to connect "Entity Data 2" to the "R" (or "Right") input anchor of the "Join" tool.

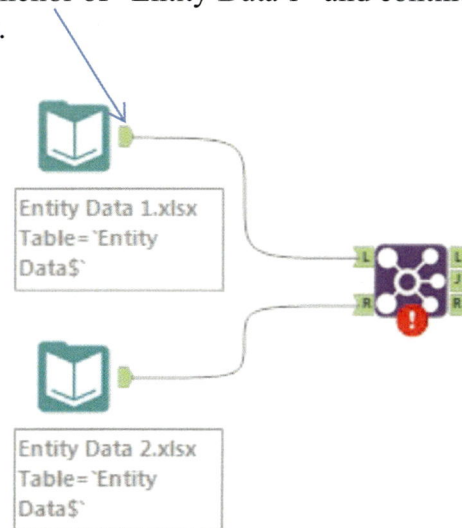

- The red exclamation point in the illustration above means the "Join" tool needs to be configured. To do so, click on it and you will see the following in the Configuration Window.

- The default option to "Join [two datasets] by Specific Fields" is the most common approach, and that's what we'll focus on in this example.
    - o Recall that throughout this book, I've been hammering away at the point that the terms "columns" and "fields" are synonymous in Alteryx.
    - o Thus, "Join by Specific Fields" means that we intend to combine two different datasets based on a single FIELD (or *column*) that they have in common.

- o This "bridge" column, the column that contains similar data in both datasets, is the "key" we will use to extract data from the secondary dataset and "blend" it into the primary dataset.

- After evaluating the two datasets, we determine that a column with entity numbers is something that both have in common. Therefore, our configuration is as follows.

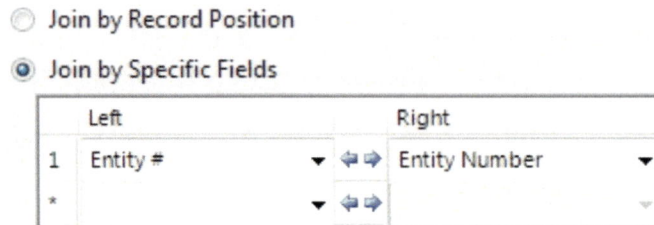

- For the "Join" configuration to successfully blend data, it's NOT necessary for the columns in the separate datasets we're keying on to have the EXACT same name.
  - o For example, in our datasets:
    - ▪ "Entity Data 1" uses the column heading "Entity #" for entity numbers and
    - ▪ "Entity Data 2" uses the column heading "Entity Number" to list the same information.
  - o What IS important is that both columns in their respective datasets contain the SAME kind of information.
    - ▪ For example, in our case both sets of data use a 5-character entity code (E0100) to identify the company named "One Hundred."
  - o It's also necessary that the data in the columns we've selected have the *same* data type.
    - ▪ In our example, the columns "Entity #" and "Entity Number" are both categorized as "V_String" (or text) data types.
    - ▪ As we learned previously, the "Select" tool can be used to adjust column data types if needed.

- Following is an illustration of the remainder of the "Join" tool's configuration.

[This space was intentionally left blank].

	Input	Field	Type		Size	Rename	Description
✓	Left	Entity Number	V_String	▾	255		
✓	Left	EIN	V_String	▾	255		
✓	Left	State	V_String	▾	255		
✓	Left	Headcount	Double	▾	8		
✓	Left	Total Assets	Double	▾	8		
✓	Left	Functional Currency	V_String	▾	255		
✓	Right	Entity #	V_String	▾	255		
✓	Right	Entity Name	V_String	▾	255		
✓	Right	Functional Currency	V_String	▾	255	Right_Functional Currency	
✓	Right	Country	V_String	▾	255		
✓	Right	Office Location	V_String	▾	255		
✓	Right	Contact	V_String	▾	255		
✓	Right	Total Sales	Double	▾	8		
✓		*Unknown	Unknown	▾	0		Dynamic or Unknown Fields

- The text in the "Field" column shows the columns that exist in each dataset.
  - Those labled "Left" are the columns that exist in the primary dataset ("Entity Data 1").
  - Those labled "Right" are the columns that exist in the secondary dataset ("Entity Data 2").
  - Note that the column "Functional Currency" has EXACTLY the same column name in both datasets.
    - When this occurs, Alteryx automatically renames the column in the secondary dataset as "Right_[Column Name]."
      - This is done so you can distinguish which dataset the "Functional Currency" information is coming from in the "Join" tool's output.
      - The red-shaded cell is also a reminder that you might want to exlude that column from your output since it contains duplicate information.

- It's also noteworthy in the illustration above that you can use the "Join" tool in a manner similar to the "Select" tool to rename, reorder and exclude columns from your output.
  - HOWEVER, as I previously recommended, I belive it's a best practice to use each tool for its primary purpose.
  - In the present case, to make our workflow visually easier to understand and to follow, we will:
    - Use the "Join" tool without further modifications to blend our data and
    - We will then follow with the "Select" tool to rename, reorder and exclude columns from our output as needed.

- With these principles and techniques in mind, we run our workflow. After it processes, we click on the ""J" output anchor on the right side of the "Join" tool.

- After doing do, in the Results Window shows what's below.[25]

Entity Number	EIN	State	Headcount	Total Assets	Functional Currency	Entity #	Entity Name
1 E0050	00-0005555	KS	282	7000000	USD	E0050	Fifty
2 E0100	10-1111000	NY	60	1500000	USD	E0100	One Hundred
3 E0200	22-2222222	CA	74	1800000	USD	E0200	Two Hundred
4 E0300	33-3333333	TX	804	20000000	USD	E0300	Three Hundred
5 E0700	77-7777777	NC	27	750000	USD	E0700	Seven Hundred
6 E0800	88-8888888	FL	83	2075000	USD	E0800	Eight Hundred
7 E0900	99-9999999	WA	162	4050000	USD	E0900	Nine Hundred
8 E1100	11-1111111	GA	325	8575000	USD	E1100	Eleven Hundred

- As I have reinterated throughtout this chapter, the "Join" tool is used to BLEND data from a secondary dataset into a primary dataset. To further clarify what this means in the context of our example:
   o In the illustation above, we see ALL entity data from the primary dataset.
   o For the secondary dataset,
      ▪ Its entity data is added to (or combined with) that of the primary dataset,
      ▪ But ONLY for those entities in the secondary dataset that are ALSO in the primary dataset.[26]

Use the "Select" tool to clean and organize "joined" data

- As I alluded to before, while the use of the "Join" tool certainly appears to have been successful, it's immediately clear that we need to use the "Select" tool to further refine our output.

- For example, referring to the illustration above:
   o We've got an "Entity Number" *and* an "Entity #" column.
      ▪ One of these can be excluded from the output.
   o Some reordering of the columns would also be helpful.
      ▪ As one example, it would be more intuitive to have the "Entity Name" column appear beside the "Entity Number" column.

- To do this cleanup, drag a "Select" tool to the Canvas and connect it to the "Join" tool's "J" output anchor (as shown in the illustration that follows).

---

[25] You would need to scroll further to the right in the Results Window to see the remainder of the blended data, but it's not important to see all of it for purposes of this example.

[26] If this is a little confusing for now, continue with the chapter and it will become clearer.

- o Again, it's very important to connect the "Select" tool to the "J" output anchor.
  - o I'll soon explain the significance of the "Join" tool's "L" and "R" output anchors.

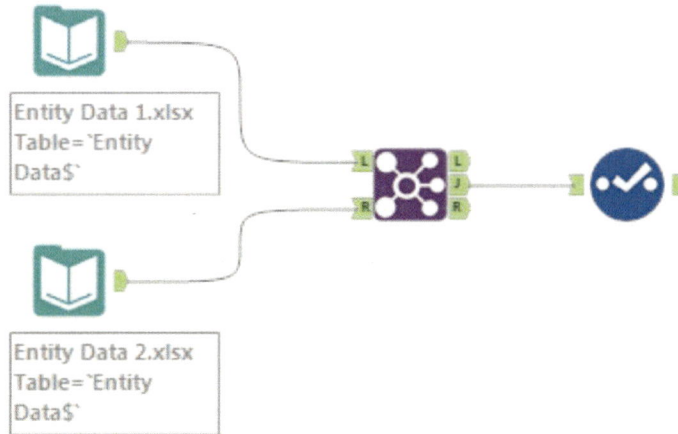

- • We'll configure the "Select" tool as follows to pare down the data to what we want to see, as well as the the the order in which we want to see it.

	Field	Type		Size	Rename	Description
☑	Entity #	V_String	▾	255		
☑	Entity Name	V_String	▾	255		
☑	EIN	V_String	▾	255		
☑	Office Location	V_String	▾	255	City	
☑	State	V_String	▾	255		
☑	Total Sales	Double	▾	8		
☑	Total Assets	Double	▾	8		
☑	Headcount	Double	▾	8		
☑	Contact	V_String	▾	255		
☐	Entity Number	V_String	▾	255		
☐	Functional Currency	V_String	▾	255		
☐	Right_Functional Currency	V_String	▾	255		
☐	Country	V_String	▾	255		
☑	*Unknown	Unknown	▾	0		Dynamic or Unknown Fields

- • To summarize some of what we did:
  - o We changed the name of the "Office Location" column to "City."
  - o We're excluding the unchecked fields (or columns) from our output (Entity Number, Right_Functional Currency and Country).

- o We reordered the columns to appear in a more logical order.

- After the above changes and running the workflow, the blended output from "Entity Data 1" and "Entity Data 2" is much cleaner, and show in the illustration that follows.

	Entity #	Entity Name	EIN	City	State	Total Sales	Total Assets	Headcount	Contact
1	E0050	Fifty	00-0005555	Kansas City	KS	19740000	7000000	282	Andy
2	E0100	One Hundred	10-1111000	New York	NY	4200000	1500000	60	Bill
3	E0200	Two Hundred	22-2222222	Los Angelas	CA	5180000	1800000	74	Martha
4	E0300	Three Hundred	33-3333333	Houston	TX	56280000	20000000	804	Nancy
5	E0700	Seven Hundred	77-7777777	Raleigh	NC	1890000	750000	27	Tony
6	E0800	Eight Hundred	88-8888888	Miami	FL	5810000	2075000	83	Michael
7	E0900	Nine Hundred	99-9999999	Seattle	WA	11340000	4050000	162	Aaron
8	E1100	Eleven Hundred	11-1111111	Atlanta	GA	19740000	8575000	325	Barbara

- To summarize, you've used data from the secondary entity dataset to add to and enhance the data in your primary dataset, but only in instances where the entities in the "Enity #" column existed in BOTH datasets.
  - o For example, our new dataset above has an "Entity Name" column.
  - o We also have information on "Total Sales."

The "Join" tool also identifies data that is NOT common to two datasets

- As a review, clicking on the "J" output anchor of the "Join" tool tells us what data was blended from our datasets.
  - o While this is important, we can also learn very useful information by from the "L" and "R" output anchors.

A review of the Left ("L") output anchor the the "Join" tool

- To illustrate this point, when we click on the "L" (or "Left") output anchor of the "Join" tool you, we see the following.

	Entity Number	EIN	State	Headcount	Total Assets	Functional Currency
1	E0010	12-3456789	DE	1	100	USD

- This shows that the Delaware holding company entity (E0010) is ONLY in the primary ("L") dataset, but it is NOT present in the secondary ("R") global entity dataset.
  - o The global group would find this very helpful to know, because it means they're missing an entity in their data!
  - o Being in the "L" anchor's output also means that Entity E0010 wasn't in BOTH datasets, therefore it's NOT part of the combined ("J") output.
    - This is a *vitally* important point to understand for the reasons that follow.

- In our example, the primary goal from the beginning was to blend data from the secondary (global) dataset into the primary (US) dataset to:
  - Created an updated list of ALL US entities with
  - More complete and robust information for each entity.

- We 've accomplished the second goal by using the "Join" tool to add more information for each entity.
  - HOWEVER, what the "L" output anchor is telling us is that a US entity – E0010 – is MISSING from our combined data.[27]
  - As a result, if we don't add entity E0010's information to our combined list, our US entity information will be *incomplete*![28]

A review of the Right ("R") output anchor the the "Join" tool

- Now click on the "R" output anchor of the "Join" tool.

	Entity #	Entity Name	Functional Currency	Country	Office Location	Contact	Total Sales
1	E0400	Four Hundred	EUR	Switzerland	Bern	Max	27580000
2	E0500	Five Hundred	JPY	Japan	Tokyo	Hichi	37600000
3	E0600	Six Hundred	USD	Germany	Berlin	Wally	8200000
4	E1000	One Thousand	EUR	France	Paris	Simone	16900000
5	E1200	Twelve Hundred	GBP	United Kingdom	London	Kurt	34300000

- What we see here is all of the entity data from the secondary dataset that was NOT included in the blended (or "J") output.

- This information is very helpful because it helps us makes intuitive sense of how our data was combined.
  - Remember, the primary dataset contained U.S. entities. What the output above is telling us is that the FOREIGN entities (see the "Country" column) were NOT blended with the primary dataset.

Other applications of the "Join" tool

With the power to join datasets, it's not hard to imagine the possibilities for accounting, tax, and finance professionals.

1) Following the methods outlined above, we could use the global entity database ("Entity Data 2") as our primary dataset and extract information from the US database to improve it.

---

[27] At the end of this chapter, we'll cover how to combine the use of the "Join" and "Union" tools to address this problem.

[28] This example shows that you can't just breeze through workflows believing that Alteryx will think for you. Designer only does what you tell it, so you have to pay careful attention to what your data is doing as it goes through the workflow, ensuring that your output is complete, accurate, and meets your needs and expectations.

2) We could combine financial data from two different ERP systems that have different headings and formats.
   o But the "Union" tool is likely a better choice, which is something we'll cover shortly.

3) In computing the R&D tax credit, you could compare two large sets of employees to determine that they're consistently categorized as R&D personnel in both datasets (and use the "L" and "R" outputs from the "Join" tool to investigate inconsistencies).

4) You can compare two trial balances to see which accounts they have in common, and which are unique.

And the possibilities go on and on!

10.4 Using the "Union" Tool to Combine <u>Uniform</u> Data from Different Sources

The Purpose of the "Union" Tool

- The purpose of the "Union" tool is to combine data from different sources (such as different Excel files) by "stacking" the datasets on top of each other.

- The difference between "stacking" data with the "Union" tool vs. "blending" it with the "Join" tool will become clear in the examples and illustrations that follow.

An example of uniform datasets that we want to combine

- To illustrate how to use the "Union" tool, let's assume that you want to combine two sets of sales data into one combined Excel file for further computations and analysis.

- The first set of date below is called "Sales Data – ERP 1.1" and, after you bring it into Alteryx with an "Input Data" tool, it looks like this.

	Transaction Date	Product	Sales Price	Credit Card	Country	State	City	Date Account Created	Last Login
1	2009-01-02 06:17:00	Product1	1200	Mastercard	United Kingdom	England	Basildon	2009-01-02 06:00:00	2009-01-02 06:08:00
2	2009-01-02 04:53:00	Product1	1200	Visa	United States	MO	Parkville	2009-01-02 04:42:00	2009-01-02 07:49:00
3	2009-01-02 13:08:00	Product1	1200	Mastercard	United States	OR	Astoria	2009-01-01 16:21:00	2009-01-03 12:32:00
4	2009-01-03 14:44:00	Product1	1200	Visa	Australia	Victoria	Echuca	2005-09-25 21:13:00	2009-01-03 14:22:00
5	2009-01-04 12:56:00	Product2	3600	Visa	United States	AL	Cahaba Heights	2008-11-15 15:47:00	2009-01-04 12:45:00

- The second set of data, called "Sales Data – ERP 1.2," looks like this.

	Transaction Date	Product	Sales Price	Credit Card	Country	State	City	Date Account Created	Last Login
1	2009-01-29 13:25:00	Product1	1200	Diners	United States	NY	Albany	2005-11-03 18:14:00	2009-02-28 08:27:00
2	2009-01-28 11:19:00	Product1	1200	Visa	United States	CO	Morrison	2004-06-20 17:16:00	2009-02-28 17:18:00
3	2009-01-07 17:48:00	Product1	1200	Mastercard	United States	GA	Augusta	2005-06-10 20:25:00	2009-02-28 19:57:00
4	2009-01-07 19:48:00	Product2	3600	Mastercard	Australia	New South Wales	Sydney	2008-09-21 20:49:00	2009-03-01 00:14:00
5	2009-01-01 04:24:00	Product3	7500	Amex	United States	NY	Skaneateles	2008-12-28 17:28:00	2009-03-01 07:21:00

- Here are some observations about these datasets.
    - They both come from ERP System #1.
    - The first dataset is from Company #1, hence the name "Sales Data – ERP 1.1."
    - The second dataset is from Company #2, hence the name "Sales Data – ERP 1.2."
    - Because the datasets come from the same ERP system, they both have the EXACT same headings and format.
    - In this simple example, each datasets contains five separate sales transactions.
        - They could each have 5,000 (or even 500,000) lines of data but, as with other examples, I'm keeping it simple so that it's easier to follow what's going on.

- To summarize, the format of both datasets in this opening example are _uniform_ in every respect EXCEPT for the fact that they reside in two different Excel files.

Using the "Union" tool to combine uniform datasets

- Now that we've imported both sales datasets into Alteryx (see the "Input Data" tools), we'll start the process of combining them by dragging a "Union" tool to the Canvas.

- The exclamation point on the "Union" tool indicates that our sales data needs to be connected to it.
    - Do this by clicking on the output anchor of "Sales Data – ERP 1.1" and dragging the black connecting line to the input anchor of the "Union" tool.
    - Follow the same process to connect "Sales Data – ERP 1.2" to the "Union" tool.

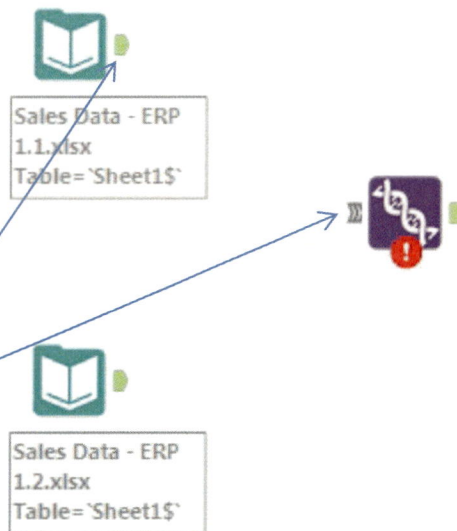

Sales Data - ERP 1.1.xlsx
Table=`Sheet1$`

Sales Data - ERP 1.2.xlsx
Table=`Sheet1$`

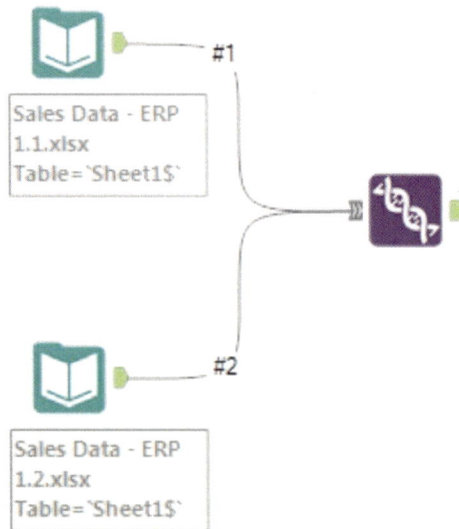

Sales Data - ERP
1.1.xlsx
Table=`Sheet1$`

#1

Sales Data - ERP
1.2.xlsx
Table=`Sheet1$`

#2

○ After you've done this, your workflow will look like the picture to the left.

• The black connection lines are numbered #1 and #2 based on the order the "Input Data" tools were connected to the "Join" tool.

○ This is significant because these numbers determine the order in which the data will be listed in the combined dataset.

○ In this specific example, the numbering means that the data in "Sales Data – ERP 1.1" will be "stacked" in the final output on top of (or appear before) the data in "Sales Data – ERP 1.2."

• After clicking on the "Union" tool, you will see the following in its configuration window.

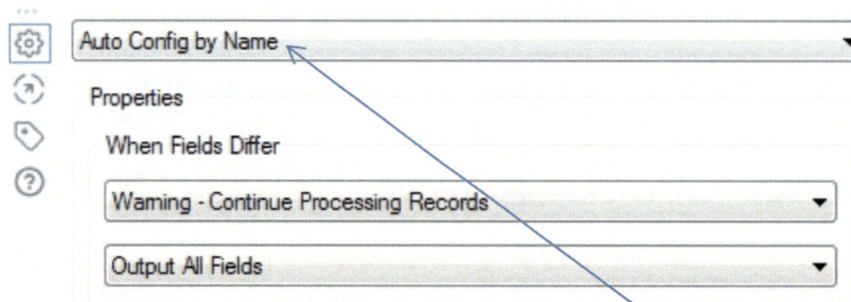

Auto Config by Name

Properties

When Fields Differ

Warning - Continue Processing Records

Output All Fields

• Your three options to combine data are:
  1) "Auto Config by Name."
     a. This is the default, and the option that's presently chosen.
  2) "Auto Config by Position."
  3) "Manually Configure Fields."[29]

• If we make no changes and run the workflow as it's presently configured, the output will look like this.

---

[29] This option will not be covered in this material, but it's good to know it exists if you have an unusual situation that you need to address.

	Transaction Date	Product	Sales Price	Credit Card	Country	State	City	Date Account Created	Last Login
1	2009-01-02 06:17:00	Product1	1200	Mastercard	United Kingdom	England	Basildon	2009-01-02 06:00:00	2009-01-02 06:08:00
2	2009-01-02 04:53:00	Product1	1200	Visa	United States	MO	Parkville	2009-01-02 04:42:00	2009-01-02 07:49:00
3	2009-01-02 13:08:00	Product1	1200	Mastercard	United States	OR	Astoria	2009-01-01 16:21:00	2009-01-03 12:32:00
4	2009-01-03 14:44:00	Product1	1200	Visa	Australia	Victoria	Echuca	2005-09-25 21:13:00	2009-01-03 14:22:00
5	2009-01-04 12:56:00	Product2	3600	Visa	United States	AL	Cahaba Heights	2008-11-15 15:47:00	2009-01-04 12:45:00
6	2009-01-29 13:25:00	Product1	1200	Diners	United States	NY	Albany	2005-11-03 18:14:00	2009-02-28 08:27:00
7	2009-01-28 11:19:00	Product1	1200	Visa	United States	CO	Morrison	2004-06-20 17:16:00	2009-02-28 17:18:00
8	2009-01-07 17:48:00	Product1	1200	Mastercard	United States	GA	Augusta	2005-06-10 20:25:00	2009-02-28 19:57:00
9	2009-01-07 19:48:00	Product2	3600	Mastercard	Australia	New South Wales	Sydney	2008-09-21 20:49:00	2009-03-01 00:14:00
10	2009-01-01 04:24:00	Product3	7500	Amex	United States	NY	Skaneateles	2008-12-28 17:28:00	2009-03-01 07:21:00

- Following are key items to note about the combined data above.
  - It's in exactly the same format as each of the standalone datasets.
    - Specifically, the names and positions of the columns in the combined data are the same as they are in the separate datasets.
  - The sales data from "Sales Data – ERP 1.1" appears in the first five lines of the combined data.
    - As noted above, this sales data appears first because its numbered connection with respect to the "Union" tool is "#1."
    - This first set of sales data is "stacked" on top of the data coming from ""Sales Data – ERP 1.2."
  - There are ten lines in the combined dataset, which represents the *total* of the five sales transactions from the two different datasets.
    - Note how "Union" tool combined (or "stacked") the data from the two sources vs. "blending" it.
    - Said another way, the combined dataset produced by the "Union" tool contains ALL the separate sales records from Company #1 and Company #2.

- If we change the configuration to "Auto Config by Position," we get the following output.

	Transaction Date	Product	Sales Price	Credit Card	Country	State	City	Date Account Created	Last Login
1	2009-01-02 06:17:00	Product1	1200	Mastercard	United Kingdom	England	Basildon	2009-01-02 06:00:00	2009-01-02 06:08:00
2	2009-01-02 04:53:00	Product1	1200	Visa	United States	MO	Parkville	2009-01-02 04:42:00	2009-01-02 07:49:00
3	2009-01-02 13:08:00	Product1	1200	Mastercard	United States	OR	Astoria	2009-01-01 16:21:00	2009-01-03 12:32:00
4	2009-01-03 14:44:00	Product1	1200	Visa	Australia	Victoria	Echuca	2005-09-25 21:13:00	2009-01-03 14:22:00
5	2009-01-04 12:56:00	Product2	3600	Visa	United States	AL	Cahaba Heights	2008-11-15 15:47:00	2009-01-04 12:45:00
6	2009-01-29 13:25:00	Product1	1200	Diners	United States	NY	Albany	2005-11-03 18:14:00	2009-02-28 08:27:00
7	2009-01-28 11:19:00	Product1	1200	Visa	United States	CO	Morrison	2004-06-20 17:16:00	2009-02-28 17:18:00
8	2009-01-07 17:48:00	Product1	1200	Mastercard	United States	GA	Augusta	2005-06-10 20:25:00	2009-02-28 19:57:00
9	2009-01-07 19:48:00	Product2	3600	Mastercard	Australia	New South Wales	Sydney	2008-09-21 20:49:00	2009-03-01 00:14:00
10	2009-01-01 04:24:00	Product3	7500	Amex	United States	NY	Skaneateles	2008-12-28 17:28:00	2009-03-01 07:21:00

- This output is the same as that produced by the "Auto Config by Name."
  - This shows that the "Union" tool's configuration doesn't matter when the data coming into it is in *exactly the same format*.
  - The differences between the "Auto Config by Name" and "Auto Config by Position," and when this configuration DOES matter will be illustrated in example in the next section.

The advantages of combining data with "Union" vs. using copy and paste in Excel

- You may ask, "Why am I using Alteryx for something as simple as combining data from two uniform datasets?"
  - This could easily be accomplished in Excel by copying the sales data from one dataset and pasting it into the other.

- My response is that you're exactly right, using Excel as described above will work perfectly.
  - I'll also add that, in situations such as the simple example we just covered, using Excel would be the fastest and easiest approach.

- Would the answer change if both datasets had 5,000 lines apiece (as opposed to just 5 lines like our example)?
  - Probably not. Using Excel shortcut keys, it only takes a little more time and effort to copy 5,000 lines of data from one dataset to another.

- Now let's turn the "complexity dial" further to the right and say that we need to combine sales data from 15 different sources (as opposed to just 2). Does that change the answer?
  - Yes. Using Excel, it would take a fair amount of time to open 15 different files and manually use copy/paste to combine them into a "masterfile."
    - Further, if any of the source data changed in the 15 files you would have to manually fix it, something that could easily turn into a time-consuming mess that would heighten the chance for making errors.

- It would be *much faster* to combine the sales data using Alteryx by doing the following:
  - Import the 15 files into a workflow using separate "Input Data" tools.
    - This will go even faster if you use the shortcut method of *dragging* the sales files to the Canvas.[30]
  - Connect the sales data to a "Union" tool.
  - Run the workflow to automatically combine all 15 sales files into a single file.
  - In addition, if any of the source data changes then you can quickly, easily, and accurately update the combined data using Alteryx by doing the following.
    - Switch out the sales data file that changed, re-run the workflow and…BAM…you're done!

---

[30] See "A shortcut – Drag source data files directly to the Canvas" on page 29 to review how this is done.

10.5 Using the "Union" Tool to Combine <u>NON</u>-Uniform Data from Different Sources

The "Union" tool can also combine non-uniform datasets

- Hopefully my explanations, examples and commentary in the previous section helped you to see the value of using Alteryx vs. Excel when combining *uniform* datasets.

- If you're not entirely sold then I can understand, especially if you've used Excel for a long time and you're comfortable with it.

- However, combing *non-uniform* datasets is an entirely different ballgame, and Alteryx is hands-down a vastly superior tool compared with Excel for doing so.

The problem of non-uniform data within organizations

- In the example in the previous section, it was straightforward to combined sales data that came from the *same* ERP system that was in the *exact same format*.

- However, what if you need to add more sales data to your combined file, but it's in a *completely different format*?

- First, is that realistic? Why would a company have sales data in different formats? A few common examples are:
  - Region #1 (the U.S. companies) uses one ERP system and Region #2 (non-U.S. affiliates) uses another.
  - To avoid the problems that can stem from this, Company A has consistently maintained a policy that all affiliates must house their financial data in ERP System #1. However:
    - Company A recently acquired Company B.
    - Company B has used ERP System #2 for many years.
    - Senior management makes a decision that Company B's *historical* financial data (including sales data) will remain in ERP System #2.
    - In addition, it will take several quarters (not to mention a mountain of effort by the IT Group) before Company B's go-forward financial operations can be cut over to ERP System #1.

- In summary, no matter how hard organizations may try to have uniform data (which is a worthy goal), it rarely works out that way due to the changing nature and complexities of business operations.
  - Given this reality, it's important to learn how to deal with non-uniform data, and Alteryx is an excellent tool to do so.

An example of non-uniform datasets

- As a reminder, the combined sales data from the previous example looked like this.

	Transaction Date	Product	Sales Price	Credit Card	Country	State	City	Date Account Created	Last Login
1	2009-01-02 06:17:00	Product1	1200	Mastercard	United Kingdom	England	Basildon	2009-01-02 06:00:00	2009-01-02 06:08:00
2	2009-01-02 04:53:00	Product1	1200	Visa	United States	MO	Parkville	2009-01-02 04:42:00	2009-01-02 07:49:00
3	2009-01-02 13:08:00	Product1	1200	Mastercard	United States	OR	Astoria	2009-01-01 16:21:00	2009-01-03 12:32:00
4	2009-01-03 14:44:00	Product1	1200	Visa	Australia	Victoria	Echuca	2005-09-25 21:13:00	2009-01-03 14:22:00
5	2009-01-04 12:56:00	Product2	3600	Visa	United States	AL	Cahaba Heights	2008-11-15 15:47:00	2009-01-04 12:45:00
6	2009-01-29 13:25:00	Product1	1200	Diners	United States	NY	Albany	2005-11-03 18:14:00	2009-02-28 08:27:00
7	2009-01-28 11:19:00	Product1	1200	Visa	United States	CO	Morrison	2004-06-20 17:16:00	2009-02-28 17:18:00
8	2009-01-07 17:48:00	Product1	1200	Mastercard	United States	GA	Augusta	2005-06-10 20:25:00	2009-02-28 19:57:00
9	2009-01-07 19:48:00	Product2	3600	Mastercard	Australia	New South Wales	Sydney	2008-09-21 20:49:00	2009-03-01 00:14:00
10	2009-01-01 04:24:00	Product3	7500	Amex	United States	NY	Skaneateles	2008-12-28 17:28:00	2009-03-01 07:21:00

- The sales data that we want to add looks like this.

	Date	Prod. Descrip.	Sale Amount	Promotion	Credit Card	Country	State/Territ...	City
1	2009-01-04	Product1	1200	N	Visa	United States	NJ	Mickleton
2	2009-01-04	Product1	3600	N	Mastercard	United States	IL	Peoria
3	2009-01-02	Product1	1200	N	Mastercard	United States	TN	Martin
4	2009-01-04	Product1	4800	Y	Visa	France	Ile-de-France	Chatou
5	2009-01-05	Product1	1200	N	Diners	United States	NY	New York

- As you can plainly see, there are numerous differences in the formats of these datasets.
  - The date columns have different names, and the dates are even in different formats.
  - The product description, sales and state columns have different names.
  - The order of the columns in the datasets is different.
  - There are columns in each dataset that don't exist in the other.

- In summary, it's true that the datasets from the different ERP both contain core sales data that we need for Excel calculations and analysis.
  - However, combining them manually in Excel would be a *disaster* in terms of effort it would take (assuming we're dealing with large datasets vs. the small sample ones above).
    - Further, the manual, tedious and time-consuming nature of the work would increase the possibility of error that comes with the territory of any labor-intensive manual process.
  - Fortunately, we can employ Alteryx's "Union" tool to combine *non-uniform* datasets such as this much more quickly and reliably.

How to use the "Union" tool to combine non-uniform datasets

- The first step in combining non-uniform data is to drag each separate dataset to the Canvas and to connect them to the "Union" tool.
  - This illustrates a *key difference* between the "Union" and the "Join" tools.

o "Join" can only be used to "blend" _two_ datasets, whereas "Union" can be used to "stack" _many_ different datasets.

- For the next step, we'll assume that we want to the column (or field) names for our output to be consistent with ERP System #1 (since that's the ERP system the acquiring company uses).[31]
    o This means that we need to use the "Select" tool to update various column names in the file "Sales Data – ERP 2.1" so they align with the column names used by Company #1 and Company #2.
    o The "Select" tool's configuration should be as follows (taking special note of the "Rename" column).

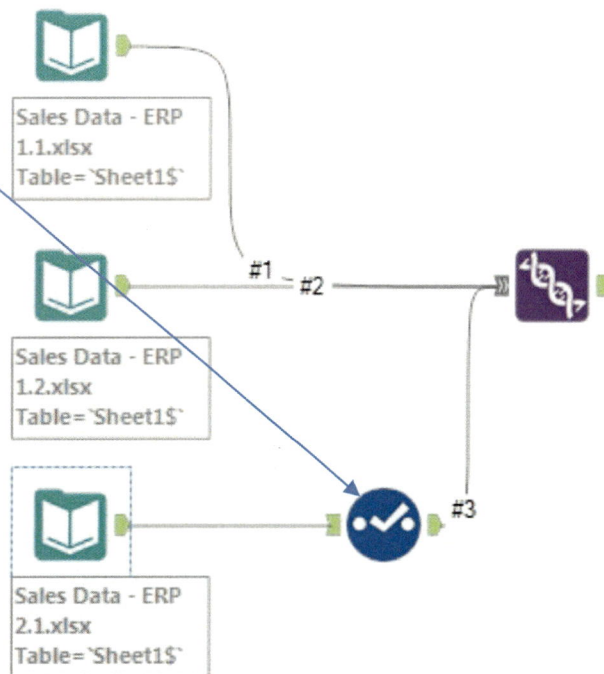

	Field	Type		Size	Rename	Description
✓	Date	Date	▾	10	Transaction Date	
✓	Prod. Descrip.	V_String	▾	255	Product	
✓	Sale Amount	Double	▾	8	Sales Price	
✓	Promotion	V_String	▾	255		
✓	Credit Card	V_String	▾	255		
✓	Country	V_String	▾	255		
✓	State/Territory	V_String	▾	255	State	
✓	City	V_String	▾	255		

Options ▾ | ↑ ↓   TIP: To reorder multiple rows: select, right-click and drag.

- With key column names in all three datasets now aligned using the "Select" tool, we're ready to start the process of combining the sales data of the three companies by adding the "Union" tool to the Canvas.
    o After connecting the sales data to the "Union" tool, the workflow will look like what's pictured to the right.

- When you're combining non-uniform data, the order in which you connect datasets to the "Union" tool _matters_.

Sales Data - ERP 1.1.xlsx
Table=`Sheet1$`

Sales Data - ERP 1.2.xlsx
Table=`Sheet1$`

Sales Data - ERP 2.1.xlsx
Table=`Sheet1$`

#1 #2 #3

---

[31] The dominant company in the merger will call the shots!

- The first dataset you connect ("#1") to the "Union" tool will drive both the NAME and ORDER of the columns in the output.
- In our example, we're using the format of "Sales Data – ERP 1.1" as the standard for our output.

- With all the data we want to combine connected to the "Union" tool, we'll now configure it by clicking on it.

  Union (5) - Configuration

  ⚙ Auto Config by Name

  - The default setting is "Auto Config by Name," and this is what we want.
  - The "Auto Config by Name" configuration combines data as follows.
    - As noted above, "Sales Data – ERP 1.1" ("Dataset #1") drives the NAME and ORDER of the columns in the output.
    - Following this logic, the sales data in Dataset #1 is added by the "Union" tool to the combined data exactly as it appears in dataset #1.
    - Recall that the dataset "Sales Data – ERP 1.2" ("Dataset #2") is in the exact same format as Dataset #1.
      - As a result, it causes NO new columns to be added to the combined data.
        - This means the sales data of Dataset #2 is stacked in the combined sales data output in EXACTLY the same manner as dataset #1.
    - With respect to "Sales Data – ERP 2.1" ("Dataset #3"):
      - It came into the workflow in an entirely different format than Datasets #1 and #2.
      - We used the "Select" tool to change various column names in Dataset #3 to match Datasets #1 and #2.
    - To the extent that Dataset #3 column names align with Dataset #1:
      - Dataset #3 data appears in the same column as Dataset #1.
      - For this to happen (which is what we want), the column names in the two datasets must be EXACTLY the same.
      - If the columns in the two datasets are not in the same order, the data in Dataset #3 will automatically shift to align with Dataset #1.
    - To the extent that Dataset #3 column names do NOT align with Dataset #1:
      - A NEW column is created at the far right of the combined data.
  - After running the workflow, a (tiny) summary of the Union tool's output is as follows.

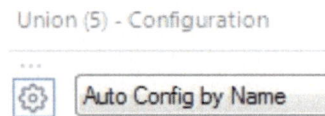

	Transaction Date	Product	Sales Price	Credit Card	Country	State	City	Date Account Crea...	Last Login	Promotion
1	2009-01-02 06:17:00	Product1	1200	Mastercard	United Kingdom	England	Basildon	2009-01-02 06:00:00	2009-01-02 06:08:00	[Null]
2	2009-01-02 04:53:00	Product1	1200	Visa	United States	MO	Parkville	2009-01-02 04:42:00	2009-01-02 07:49:00	[Null]
.3	2009-01-02 13:08:00	Product1	1200	Mastercard	United States	OR	Astoria	2009-01-01 16:21:00	2009-01-03 12:32:00	[Null]
4	2009-01-03 14:44:00	Product1	1200	Visa	Australia	Victoria	Echuca	2005-09-25 21:13:00	2009-01-03 14:22:00	[Null]
5	2009-01-04 12:56:00	Product2	3600	Visa	United States	AL	Cahaba Heights	2008-11-15 15:47:00	2009-01-04 12:45:00	[Null]
6	2009-01-04	Product1	1200	Visa	United States	NJ	Mickleton	[Null]	[Null]	N
7	2009-01-04	Product1	3600	Mastercard	United States	IL	Peoria	[Null]	[Null]	N
8	2009-01-02	Product1	1200	Mastercard	United States	TN	Martin	[Null]	[Null]	N
9	2009-01-04	Product1	4800	Visa	France	Ile-de-France	Chatou	[Null]	[Null]	Y
10	2009-01-05	Product1	1200	Diners	United States	NY	New York	[Null]	[Null]	N
11	2009-01-29 13:25:00	Product1	1200	Diners	United States	NY	Albany	2005-11-03 18:14:00	2009-02-28 08:27:00	[Null]
12	2009-01-28 11:19:00	Product1	1200	Visa	United States	CO	Morrison	2004-06-20 17:16:00	2009-02-28 17:18:00	[Null]
13	2009-01-07 17:48:00	Product1	1200	Mastercard	United States	GA	Augusta	2005-06-10 20:25:00	2009-02-28 19:57:00	[Null]
14	2009-01-07 19:48:00	Product2	3600	Mastercard	Australia	New South Wales	Sydney	2008-09-21 20:49:00	2009-03-01 00:14:00	[Null]
15	2009-01-01 04:24:00	Product3	7500	Amex	United States	NY	Skaneateles	2008-12-28 17:28:00	2009-03-01 07:21:00	[Null]

- Some observations of the combined output are:
  - There are 15 lines of data, which makes sense, because it's the total of all of lines of data in the three datasets.
  - Null values populated where data for a given column doesn't exist.
    - For example, Dataset #3 is the only one with information on whether a sale was related to a product promotion (see the "Promotion" column at the far right).
    - Similarly, there is no data in Dataset #3 on the date a customer account was created, or their last login date.
  - The presentation of the date/time-related data in the "Transaction Date" column is inconsistent.

- Given these differences, we recognize that a "Select" tool should be placed after the "Union" tool to clean up the output.
  - After dragging "Select" to the workflow and configuring the tool, our final product for export to Excel looks like this.

	Transaction Date	Product	Sales Price	Credit Card	City	State	Country
1	2009-01-02	Product1	1200	Mastercard	Basildon	England	United Kingdom
2	2009-01-02	Product1	1200	Visa	Parkville	MO	United States
3	2009-01-02	Product1	1200	Mastercard	Astoria	OR	United States
4	2009-01-03	Product1	1200	Visa	Echuca	Victoria	Australia
5	2009-01-04	Product2	3600	Visa	Cahaba Heights	AL	United States
6	2009-01-04	Product1	1200	Visa	Mickleton	NJ	United States
7	2009-01-04	Product1	3600	Mastercard	Peoria	IL	United States
8	2009-01-02	Product1	1200	Mastercard	Martin	TN	United States
9	2009-01-04	Product1	4800	Visa	Chatou	Ile-de-France	France
10	2009-01-05	Product1	1200	Diners	New York	NY	United States
11	2009-01-29	Product1	1200	Diners	Albany	NY	United States
12	2009-01-28	Product1	1200	Visa	Morrison	CO	United States
13	2009-01-07	Product1	1200	Mastercard	Augusta	GA	United States
14	2009-01-07	Product2	3600	Mastercard	Sydney	New South Wales	Australia
15	2009-01-01	Product3	7500	Amex	Skaneateles	NY	United States

The "Union" tool's "Auto Config by Position" configuration

- With an understanding of how the "Auto Config by Name" configuration setting "stacks" data based on the previous example, we can now revisit the "Auto Config by Position" setting.

- As previously noted, the "Auto Config by Name" setting *automatically* aligns data in different datasets based on a column's name.

- The "Auto Config by Position" setting doesn't do ANY automatic alignment. Instead, here's how it works.
    - The dataset labeled "#1" going into the "Union" tool governs the EXACT name and order of the output columns.
    - Date from ALL datasets is stacked in that exact same order.
    - If datasets contain more columns than the first ("#1") dataset, those columns are NOT included as part of the combined data.

- With these factors in mind, if we change the previous example's configuration to "Auto Config by Position" then we get the following output.

	Transaction Date	Product	Sales Price	Credit Card	Country	State	City	Date Account Created	Last Login
1	2009-01-02 06:17:00	Product1	1200	Mastercard	United Kingdom	England	Basildon	2009-01-02 06:00:00	2009-01-02 06:08:00
2	2009-01-02 04:53:00	Product1	1200	Visa	United States	MO	Parkville	2009-01-02 04:42:00	2009-01-02 07:49:00
3	2009-01-02 13:08:00	Product1	1200	Mastercard	United States	OR	Astoria	2009-01-01 16:21:00	2009-01-03 12:32:00
4	2009-01-03 14:44:00	Product1	1200	Visa	Australia	Victoria	Echuca	2005-09-25 21:13:00	2009-01-03 14:22:00
5	2009-01-04 12:56:00	Product2	3600	Visa	United States	AL	Cahaba Heights	2008-11-15 15:47:00	2009-01-04 12:45:00
6	2009-01-04	Product1	1200	N	Visa	United States	NJ	Mickleton	[Null]
7	2009-01-04	Product1	3600	N	Mastercard	United States	IL	Peoria	[Null]
8	2009-01-02	Product1	1200	N	Mastercard	United States	TN	Martin	[Null]
9	2009-01-04	Product1	4800	Y	Visa	France	Ile-de-France	Chatou	[Null]
10	2009-01-05	Product1	1200	N	Diners	United States	NY	New York	[Null]
11	2009-01-29 13:25:00	Product1	1200	Diners	United States	NY	Albany	2005-11-03 18:14:00	2009-02-28 08:27:00
12	2009-01-28 11:19:00	Product1	1200	Visa	United States	CO	Morrison	2004-06-20 17:16:00	2009-02-28 17:18:00
13	2009-01-07 17:48:00	Product1	1200	Mastercard	United States	GA	Augusta	2005-06-10 20:25:00	2009-02-28 19:57:00
14	2009-01-07 19:48:00	Product2	3600	Mastercard	Australia	New South Wales	Sydney	2008-09-21 20:49:00	2009-03-01 00:14:00
15	2009-01-01 04:24:00	Product3	7500	Amex	United States	NY	Skaneateles	2008-12-28 17:28:00	2009-03-01 07:21:00

- At first glance the output appears to be okay, but upon closer inspection you realize it's not.
    - The "Credit Card" column has "Y" and "N" as some of the listings.
    - The "Country" column contains some credit card information.
    - We could go on, but the point is that there's a clear lack of alignment between the datasets, and that is what's causing the problems.

- In summary, "Auto Config by Position" only works when there is alignment in the data in columns for ALL datasets.

10.6 Combining the Use of "Join" and "Union" to Produced Complete and Enhanced Data

Shortcomings of using "Join" and "Union" by themselves

- Let's return to the example in this chapter where we used the "Join" tool to blend entity data.

- If you recall, there was a problem.
    - Our goal was to produce a complete and enhanced list of US entity data.
    - The "Join" did succeed in ENHANCING our entity data.
    - However, because one of the entities was not in BOTH datasets, that entity was DROPPED from our combined data.
        - Referring to the example in Section 10.3, Entity E0010 was excluded from our combined data.
        - We learned this by clicking on the "L" output anchor of the "Join" tool.
    - In summary, while the "Join" tool did not entirely "lose" the entity below, it also didn't include it as part of the final data in the "J" output anchor.

	Entity Number	EIN	State	Headcount	Total Assets	Functional Currency
1	E0010	12-3456789	DE	1	100	USD

- If ensuring we have a complete U.S. entity dataset is our goal, should we use the "Union" tool instead?
    - The logic here is that the "Union" tool will "stack" entities from combined datasets on top of one another, so no data will be lost.
    - With that in mind, we create the following workflow.

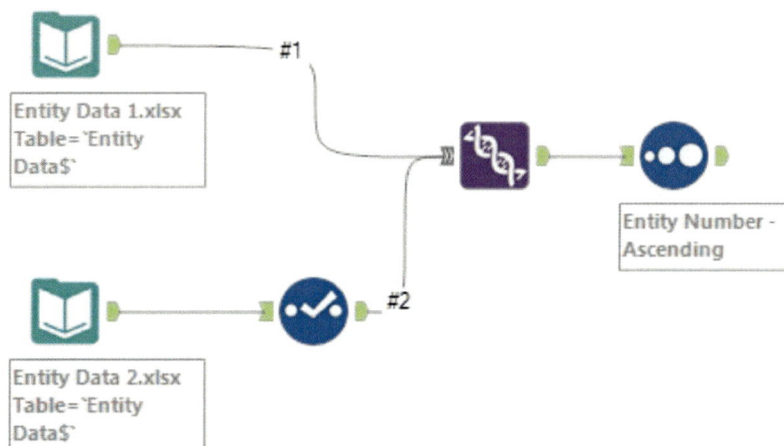

- After running the workflow, a partial view of our sorted output is as follows.

	Entity Number	EIN	State	Headcount	Total Assets	Functional Currency	Entity Name
1	E0010	12-3456789	DE	1	100	USD	[Null]
2	E0050	00-0005555	KS	282	7000000	USD	[Null]
3	E0050	[Null]	[Null]	[Null]	[Null]	USD	Fifty
4	E0100	10-1111000	NY	60	1500000	USD	[Null]
5	E0100	[Null]	[Null]	[Null]	[Null]	USD	One Hundred
6	E0200	22-2222222	CA	74	1800000	USD	[Null]
7	E0200	[Null]	[Null]	[Null]	[Null]	USD	Two Hundred
8	E0300	33-3333333	TX	804	20000000	USD	[Null]
9	E0300	[Null]	[Null]	[Null]	[Null]	USD	Three Hundred
10	E0400	[Null]	[Null]	[Null]	[Null]	EUR	Four Hundred

- Can you see the problem? We've got all the entity data from both datasets, but it's "stacked."
  - For example, there are now two rows with Entity 50, Entity 100, etc.
  - How could we combine entity rows in this format?
  - Based on what we've learned so far, the "Filter" tool comes to mind. However, that won't work because it removes rows, and we need at least some of the data on EACH of the rows above![32]

- In summary, used alone, neither the "Join" tool nor the "Union" tool provides a clean, satisfactory means to accomplish our goal.

An example of combining the "Join" and "Union" tools to produce complete AND enhanced data

- It seems like there should be a way to combine the strengths of the "Join" and "Union" tools, and the good news is that there is.
  - The first step is to go back to the workflow in Section 10.3 where we originally blended "Entity Data 1" with "Entity Data 2" (pictured to the right).

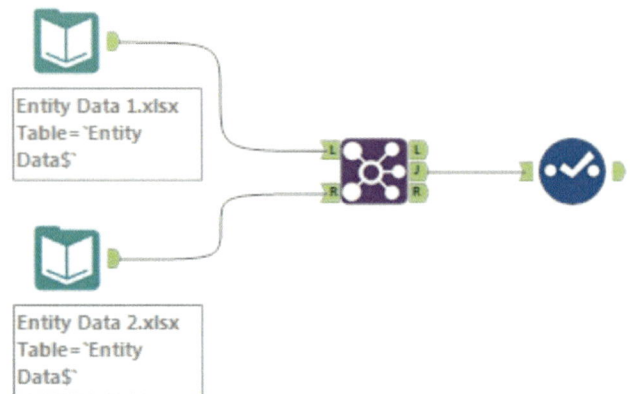

- Recall that we were happy with the enhanced output produced by this workflow, except for the fact that it was missing entity E0010.
  - How did we know this?

---

[32] Later in the book you'll also learn that the "Summarize" tool is a powerful compliment to the "Filter" tool in managing data organized in rows. However, that tool won't help us in this case, either.

o As a review, we discovered Entity E0010 wasn't in our final "joined" output by clicking on the "L" anchor of the "Join" tool.

	Entity Number	EIN	State	Headcount	Total Assets	Functional Currency
1	E0010	12-3456789	DE	1	100	USD

- Is there tool that combine these two sets of data? In other words, can we combine the data what was enhanced by the "Join" tool with the missing entity data above (E0010)?
  o The answer is yes, the "Union" tool will do the job.

- Knowing this, we first connect "Select" tools to the "Join" tool's output anchors (the "J" and "L" output anchors) so we can make the column names in the two datasets exactly the same.
  o This will allow the "Auto Config by Name" configuration of the "Union" tool to work properly.
  o After the column names are aligned, the next step is to add a "Union" tool to combine the two datasets. After following these steps, our workflow looks like this.

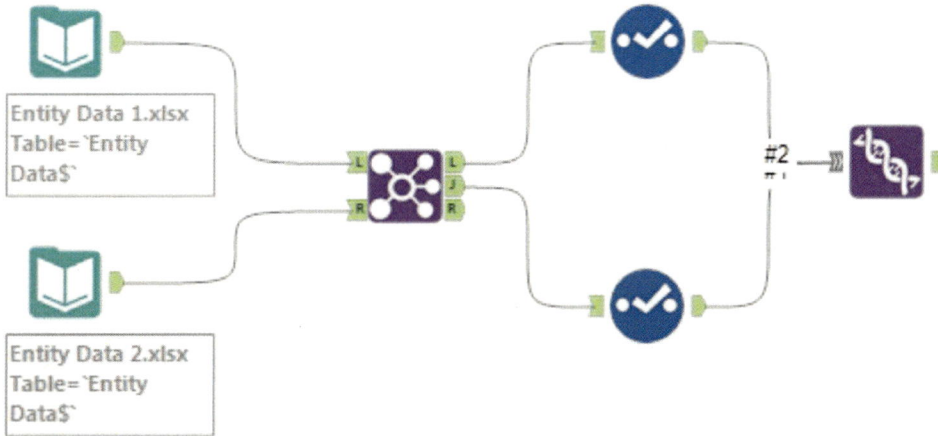

- After running the workflow, our output looks like this.

	Entity #	Entity Name	EIN	City	State	Total Sales	Total Assets	Headcount	Contact
1	E0010	[Null]	12-3456789	[Null]	DE	[Null]	100	1	[Null]
2	E0050	Fifty	00-0005555	Kansas City	KS	19740000	7000000	282	Andy
3	E0100	One Hundred	10-1111000	New York	NY	4200000	1500000	60	Bill
4	E0200	Two Hundred	22-2222222	Los Angelas	CA	5180000	1800000	74	Martha
5	E0300	Three Hundred	33-3333333	Houston	TX	56280000	20000000	804	Nancy
6	E0700	Seven Hundred	77-7777777	Raleigh	NC	1890000	750000	27	Tony
7	E0800	Eight Hundred	88-8888888	Miami	FL	5810000	2075000	83	Michael
8	E0900	Nine Hundred	99-9999999	Seattle	WA	11340000	4050000	162	Aaron
9	E1100	Eleven Hundred	11-1111111	Atlanta	GA	19740000	8575000	325	Barbara

- Notice that Entity E0010 (in the top row) is now part of our complete and enhanced dataset of U.S. entities.

- In summary, by combining the use of the "Join" and "Union" tools, we got the best of both worlds:
    - We used the "Join" tool to add to and enhance Entity Data 1 (U.S.) with the additional information from Entity Data 2 (global) AND
    - We used the "Union" tool to ensure that the new and improved Entity Data 1 dataset included data for all US entities.

11 Advanced Techniques for Manipulating Data Presented in Rows and Columns

11.1 Learning Objectives

Upon the completion of this chapter, you will:

- Understand the purposes of the "Cross" tab and the "Transform" tools, how they are related and how they are different.
- Be able to use the "Cross Tab" tool to transform columnar data to rows.
- Be able to use the "Transpose" tool to transform data presented in rows to a columnar format.
- Know how to use the "Filter" tool on conjunction with the "Transpose" tool to refine and streamline data output.

11.2 Use "Cross Tab" Tool to Transform Columnar Data to Rows

An introduction to the "Cross Tab" tool

Fundamentally, the purpose of the "Cross Tab" tool is to transform data presented in a columnar format to one based on rows.
  - This is indicated on the picture of the tool itself.

Cross Tab

- This is similar to the following Excel features.
  - Copy – Paste Special – Transpose.
  - The "Transpose" function.

- Excel can be the quickest and most efficient way to covert columnar data to rows if:
  - You're dealing with a limited amount of data
  - The data is in a simple format or
  - The cells you're transforming don't contain formulas.

- However, Alteryx is far more adept at transforming:
  - Large amounts of data and/or
  - Data that is laid out in more complex formats.

- These points are best illustrated in the commentary and examples that follow.

An example of converting data presented in columns to rows

- At present, we have sales data that's organized by entity, which is the column in the far left of the dataset below.

- We need to perform an Excel analysis that includes sales by entity. However, to do so efficiently based on how we want to do our Excel analysis, we need sales and entity data presented in rows, as shown in the illustration below.

	Entity	Parent	Sales	State	County
1	E00001	Company A	100	TX	TX-A
2	E00002	Company B	200	NC	NC-A
3	E00003	Company C	300	TX	TX-A
4	E00004	Company A	400	VT	VT-A
5	E00005	Company C	500	CA	CA-A
6	E00006	Company A	600	NC	NC-B
7	E00007	Company B	700	TX	TX-B
8	E00008	Company A	800	NY	NY-A

E00001	E00002	E00003	E00004	E00005	E00006	E00007	E00008
100	200	300	400	500	600	700	800

- How do we get there, transforming a column-based presentation to rows?

Entity Data.xlsx
Table=`Sheet1$`

- First, we go to the "Transform" section of the Tool Palette, locate the "Cross Tab" tool, and then place it onto the Canvas next to our entity data.

- Now we configure the "Cross Tab" tool is as shown in the illustration, noting the following:

  o Nothing needs to be selected (or checked) in the section "Group data by these values."
  - We will cover what impact this section has on our data shortly.

  o For "Change column headers," selecting "Entity" coverts the entity numbers as the NEW headings for ALL our columns.
  - Referring to the illustration at the top of the page, the columns were previously "Entity," "Parent," "Sales," "State" and "County."

  o "Sales" should be selected for "Values for new columns."

Group data by these values

Select All

- Entity
- Parent
- Sales
- State
- County

Change column headers

Entity

Values for new columns

Sales

Method for aggregating values

Select All

- ☑ Sum
- ☐ Average
- ☐ Count (without Nulls)

- This will take the "Sales" data originally listed in a columnar format and covert it to a row format.
  - o In the "Method for aggregating values" section of the configuration, check "Sum" to present the total amount of sales by entity.
  - o After running the workflow our output will look like this.

E00001	E00002	E00003	E00004	E00005	E00006	E00007	E00008
100	200	300	400	500	600	700	800

- Instead of sales figures, what if we needed to list the parent company name under each entity, meaning that our output should look like this:

E00001	E00002	E00003	E00004	E00005	E00006	E00007	E00008
Company A	Company B	Company C	Company A	Company C	Company A	Company B	Company A

- To accomplish this, we would change the configuration as follows.

Change column headers

Entity

Values for new columns

Parent

Method for aggregating values

☑ Concatenate

Use the "Group data by these values" configuration section to organize your data using additional columns

- What if we need to see entity sales grouped by state, pictured as follows?

	State	E00001	E00002	E00003	E00004	E00005	E00006	E00007	E00008
1	CA	[Null]	[Null]	[Null]	[Null]	500	[Null]	[Null]	[Null]
2	NC	[Null]	200	[Null]	[Null]	[Null]	600	[Null]	[Null]
3	NY	[Null]	[Null]	[Null]	[Null]	[Null]	[Null]	[Null]	800
4	TX	100	[Null]	300	[Null]	[Null]	[Null]	700	[Null]
5	VT	[Null]	[Null]	[Null]	400	[Null]	[Null]	[Null]	[Null]

- To accomplish this, we would check "State" in the section "Group data by these values."

Group data by these values

☐ Entity

☐ Parent

☐ Sales

☑ State

☐ County

- What if we needed to get even more granular, to see sales by state AND by county?
  - If we checked the "County" option above (while also keeping "State" checked) then our output would be as follows.

	State	County	E00001	E00002	E00003	E00004	E00005	E00006	E00007	E00008
1	CA	CA-A	[Null]	[Null]	[Null]	[Null]	500	[Null]	[Null]	[Null]
2	NC	NC-A	[Null]	200	[Null]	[Null]	[Null]	[Null]	[Null]	[Null]
3	NC	NC-B	[Null]	[Null]	[Null]	[Null]	[Null]	600	[Null]	[Null]
4	NY	NY-A	[Null]	[Null]	[Null]	[Null]	[Null]	[Null]	[Null]	800
5	TX	TX-A	100	[Null]	300	[Null]	[Null]	[Null]	[Null]	[Null]
6	TX	TX-B	[Null]	[Null]	[Null]	[Null]	[Null]	[Null]	700	[Null]
7	VT	VT-A	[Null]	[Null]	[Null]	400	[Null]	[Null]	[Null]	[Null]

11.3 Use the "Transpose" Tool to Convert Data Presented in Rows to a Columnar Format

An introduction to the "Cross Tab" tool

- As a companion to the "Cross Tab" tool, the purpose of the "Transpose" tool is to transform data presented in rows to a columnar format.
  - This is indicated by the picture on the tool itself.

Transpose

- This functionality will be illustrated in the commentary and examples that follow.

A simple example of converting data presented in rows to columns

- At present, we have net income data organized by entity that looks like this.

Description	Entity A	Entity B	Entity C	Entity D	Entity E	Entity F	Entity G
Net Income	100	300	200	500	400	500	600

- We need to perform an Excel analysis that includes net income by entity. However, to do so efficiently (based on how our spreadsheet is organized), we need our net income by entity presented as follows.

	Entity Name	Net Income
1	Entity A	100
2	Entity B	300
3	Entity C	200
4	Entity D	500
5	Entity E	400
6	Entity F	500
7	Entity G	600

- How we get there using Alteryx? First, we go to the "Transform" section of the Tool Palette, locate the "Transpose" tool, and then place it onto the Canvas next to our entity data.

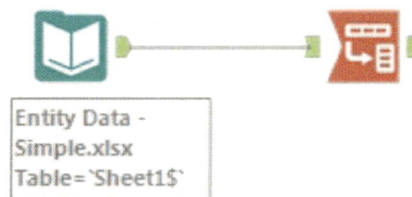

Entity Data -
Simple.xlsx
Table=`Sheet1$`

[This space was intentionally left blank].

- To transform our net income organized in rows (as pictured on the previous page) to columns, we configure the "Transpose" tool as illustrated to the right.
  - Note: The boxes for Entities E-G in the "Data columns" section should also be checked even though they are not shown in the illustration.

- Following are items to note with respect to the configuration.
  - By checking a box in the "Key columns" section, we're telling Designer that we want the information in that column to populate in rows
    - In our example, by checking the "Description" box, Alteryx will populate every row of data that's produced by the "Transpose" tool with the description "Net Income."
    - After checking "Description" in the "Key columns" section, "Description" will automatically be unchecked as an option in the "Data columns" section (described below).
  - In the "Date columns" section, we're telling Designer what columns from the data coming into the "Transpose" tool ("Entity A," "Entity B," etc.) that we want to appear as rows in the output.
    - By default, all columns are selected EXCEPT for those checked in the "Key columns" section.
  - After running the workflow, our output looks like this.

Key columns

- ☑ Description
- ☐ Entity A
- ☐ Entity B
- ☐ Entity C
- ☐ Entity D
- ☐ Entity E
- ☐ Entity F
- ☐ Entity G

	Description	Name	Value
1	Net Income	Entity A	100
2	Net Income	Entity B	300
3	Net Income	Entity C	200
4	Net Income	Entity D	500
5	Net Income	Entity E	400
6	Net Income	Entity F	500
7	Net Income	Entity G	600

Data columns

- ☐ Description
- ☑ Entity A
- ☑ Entity B
- ☑ Entity C
- ☑ Entity D

- By connecting a "Select" tool to the "Transpose" tool, we can further clean up our output by removing the "Description" column with the following configuration.
  - Note in the "Select" tool's configuration that we've unchecked the "Description" column.

	Field	Type		Size	Rename
☐	Description	V_String	▾	255	
☑	Name	String	▾	8	Entity Name
☑	Value	Double	▾	8	Net Income

- After re-running the workflow, our output will look like this.

	Entity Name	Net Income
1	Entity A	100
2	Entity B	300
3	Entity C	200
4	Entity D	500
5	Entity E	400
6	Entity F	500
7	Entity G	600

- Revisiting the "Transpose" tool's configuration illustrated on the previous page, if we had checked "Entity A" in the "Key columns" section rather than "Description," the output would have looked like this.

	Entity A	Name	Value
1	100	Entity B	300
2	100	Entity C	200
3	100	Entity D	500
4	100	Entity E	400
5	100	Entity F	500
6	100	Entity G	600

- As you can see, the output makes no sense.
    - This is because we've configured Designer to populate every row with "Entity A's" net income.
    - The point here is that *every* configuration won't produce useful data; you need to visualize what you're aiming to accomplish and configure the "Transpose" tool accordingly.

Data columns

- Going back to our base configuration with "Description" once again being checked in the "Key columns" section, how can we exclude the net income of "Entity A" from the output?
    - This can be done by unchecking the "Entity A" box in the "Data Columns" section.

☐ Description

☐ Entity A

	Entity Name	Net Income
1	Entity B	300
2	Entity C	200
3	Entity D	500
4	Entity E	400
5	Entity F	500
6	Entity G	600

- After re-running the workflow (with the addition of the "Select" tool as described above), the updated output would look like what's shown to the left (omitting "Entity A" net income).

☑ Entity B

☑ Entity C

A more complex example of using the "Transpose" tool to convert data presented in rows to columns

- To illustrate a more complex example, assume our dataset now has fewer entities, but there is more data presented on rows for each entity.

	Description	Entity A	Entity B	Entity C
1	Gross Income	100	300	200
2	Tax Rate	0.1	0.2	0.3
3	Tax	10	60	60
4	Net Income	90	240	140

- Let's first assume that we configured the "Transpose" tool exactly as we had in the last example (which is illustrated to the right).

- Based on this configuration, after re-running the workflow the output would look like this:

	Description	Name	Value
1	Gross Income	Entity A	100
2	Gross Income	Entity B	300
3	Gross Income	Entity C	200
4	Tax Rate	Entity A	0.1
5	Tax Rate	Entity B	0.2
6	Tax Rate	Entity C	0.3
7	Tax	Entity A	10
8	Tax	Entity B	60
9	Tax	Entity C	60
10	Net Income	Entity A	90
11	Net Income	Entity B	240
12	Net Income	Entity C	140

Key columns

☑ Description
☐ Entity A
☐ Entity B
☐ Entity C
☐ Entity D
☐ Entity E
☐ Entity F
☐ Entity G

Data columns

☐ Description
☑ Entity A
☑ Entity B
☑ Entity C

- Notice how the "Transpose" tool's configuration caused the output to be "stacked" by the data in the "Description" column.
  - For example, "Gross Income" is listed three times, once each for entities A, B, and C.
  - "Tax Rate" and other rows follow this same pattern.
  - Obviously, this format isn't very useful.

- What if our goal was the same as in the example in the previous subsection, to see net income by entity in a columnar format? How would we get there?
  - We would add a "Filter" tool to our workflow after the "Transpose" tool and configure the "Filter" tool as follows.

Description		Equals		Net Income

- After re-running the workflow, our output would only include rows that contained "Net Income" as shown below.

	Description	Name	Value
1	Net Income	Entity A	90
2	Net Income	Entity B	240
3	Net Income	Entity C	140

- We could then add a "Select" tool to our workflow for the additional cleanup that's described in the previous subsection.

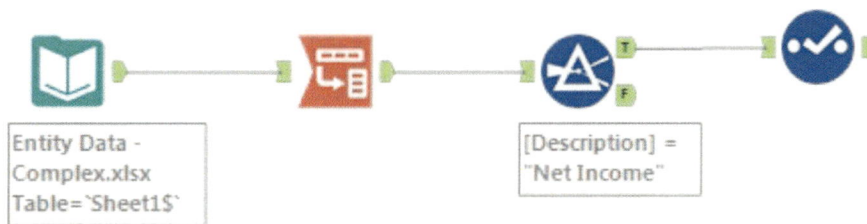

Entity Data -
Complex.xlsx
Table=`Sheet1$`

[Description] =
"Net Income"

- After re-running the workflow, the output would look like this.

	Entity Name	Net Income
1	Entity A	90
2	Entity B	240
3	Entity C	140

- Note that this is the *same* output and result as in the previous section, we just needed to do a little more work to get there (i.e., using the "Filter" tool as described above).

12 Perform Calculations and Manage Rows Using the "Summarize" Tool

12.1 Learning Objectives

Upon the completion of this chapter, you will:

- Be able to articulate Excel's advantages over Alteryx in performing calculations.
- Know how to use the "Summarize" tool to sum the figures in a dataset.
- Be able to configure the "Summarize" tool to automatically break totals (e.g., total sales) into subcategories (country, state, city, etc.).
- Learn how to use the "Summarize" tool's "Group By" capability as a powerful way to manage rows by aggregating data.
- Learn some of the "Summarize" tool's other capabilities, such as counting and averaging data.
- Identify multiple ways a "Summarize" tool can be used to prove out various figures in a workflow to improve internal controls.
- Recognize how the "Comments" tool can be used to improve SOX controls.

12.2 Performing Calculations – Excel's Advantages Over Alteryx

- Thus far, we've used Alteryx to organize, cleanse, format, blend, combine, and to otherwise manipulate data.

- However, up to this point we have <u>NOT</u> used Alteryx to perform any calculations. Following are my reasons for this.

1) I've aimed to present the material in this book in a progressive manner.
   a. I believe the first steps are to *organize* data and
   b. *Then* you can more efficiently and accurately perform calculations with that data.

2) I believe Excel is a better, more flexible, and more intuitive tool than Alteryx for performing calculations.
   a. Recall my analogy comparing Alteryx and Excel to golf clubs.[33]
      i. Alteryx is the best "club" for organizing data but
      ii. Excel is best for performing computations with that data.

---

[33] See page 10.

b. I recognize that my point of view is subjective. But I have experience using both Excel and Alteryx in complex tax projects, and I stand by my opinion.

3) Regardless of what *I* believe, most accounting, tax, and financial professionals who review your work in a corporate, Big 4, or similar environment strongly prefer to see calculations in an Excel vs. an Alteryx format.
   a. Why is this the case? No matter how powerful Alteryx may be, most reviewers are simply more familiar with Excel than Alteryx (and they may not even have an Alteryx software license!).

4) Excel is a far more flexible tool than Alteryx for documenting and referencing work.
   a. This is not to say that Alteryx cannot be a strong component of your SOX controls – I absolutely believe it can be. But I would personally find it cumbersome to exclusively rely on using Alteryx to document my work.
   b. Related to the prior point, Excel, with its "blank slate" and freehand format, enables you to develop, shape and polish work products with a high degree of precision IF you follow the right principles, methods, and practices.[34]

- In summary, I vastly prefer Excel over Alteryx for performing computations.
  - That said, I believe it's important for accounting, tax, and finance professionals to know how to use Alteryx to perform calculations.
  - Knowing how to do so will dramatically expand your capabilities with Alteryx, and it will also enable you to make an informed judgment on whether Alteryx or Excel is the right tool to use for what you're aiming to accomplish.

12.3 A Brief Review of Organizing, Formatting and Cleansing Data

- As I've stated repeatedly, it's _vitally important_ to organize, format and cleanse data as much as possible prior to using it in calculations.
  - If the maxim "garbage in, garbage out"[35] is true, then it follows that "clean data in, accurate calculations out" must also be true!

- That being the case, I believe it's worth briefly reviewing the workflow that was used to create the clean sales data for examples in this chapter.

---

[34] I recognize this is a massive "IF" given how poorly Excel work products can be when the right principles, methods and practices are NOT followed. However, a deep dive into that is beyond the scope of this book and the subject for another one.

[35] This term was coined by an early IBM programmer named George Fuechsel.

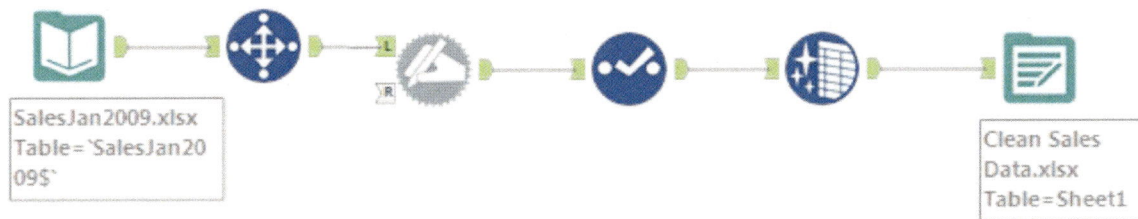

SalesJan2009.xlsx
Table=`SalesJan20
09$`

Clean Sales
Data.xlsx
Table=Sheet1

- This workflow above accomplishes the following.

  1) The "Input Data" tool is used to import raw sales data from the GL into the workflow.

  2) The "Select Records" tool is used to clean up the top portion of the raw data.

  3) "Dynamic Rename" is used to automatically populate field (or column) names.

  4) The "Select" tool is used to:
     a. Rename certain columns.
     b. Remove columns not needed in the output.
     c. Reorder columns into a logical sequence.
     d. Change the formatting of columns as needed to ensure the data types are correct (numeric, text or a date format).

  5) The "Data Cleansing" tool is used to clean up the formatting of the data.

  6) The "Output Data" tool is used to export the data to an Excel file called "Clean Sales Data."

Note: The "Clean Sales Data" Excel produced by the "Output Data" tool in Step 6 is the source data of the "Input Data" tools for all the sales-related workflow examples that follow in this chapter.

12.4 How to Configure the "Summarize" Tool and to Sum Data and to Break it into Categories

How to configure the "Summarize" tool

- The "Summarize" tool can be used to analyze data in a number of ways (detailed later in the chapter).

- The first step in doing so is to place a "Summarize" tool beside the "Input Data" that

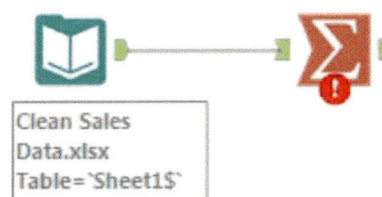

Clean Sales
Data.xlsx
Table=`Sheet1$`

contains our cleaned-up sales data, which was produced by the workflow in the previous subsection.

- The red exclamation point indicates that the "Summarize" tool needs to be configured. To do so, click on it, and you will then see the following.

Fields: Select ▼

	Field	Type
▶	Transaction Date	Date
	Product	V_String
	Sales Price	Double
	Credit Card	V_String
	Country	V_String
	State	V_String
	City	V_String
	Date Account Cr...	DateTime
	Last Login	DateTime

Actions: Add ▼

	Field	Action	Output Field Name

↑
↓
⊖

- The "Fields" section above lists:
  - All the columns (in order) of the data flowing into the "Summarize" tool.
  - It also shows the data type of each column.
    - The data type (number, text, or date) determines the actions you can perform with the "Summarize" tool on a given column.
    - If a column is NOT the correct data type (e.g., it's a V_String but needs to be a number), that's something you need to correct with a "Select" tool BEFORE the data comes into the "Summarize" tool.
  - In summary, the "Fields" section lists the full range of columns on which you can perform computations using the "Summarize" tool.

- The "Actions" section of the configuration is used to:
  - Pull in columns from the "Fields" section.
  - From there, you will select an "Action" (or computation) that you want to "Summarize" tool to perform on the column.

- o Note that you can pull down multiple columns from the "Fields" section to the "Actions" section.
  - ▪ Alteryx will perform computations on the data in in the "Actions" section in a sequential manner, starting with the top action and working down to the bottom.
  - ▪ Use the up and down arrows at the far right of the "Actions" section to change the order in which you want computations to be performed.
  - ▪ Below these arrows is a delete button which can be used to remove columns (and their related computations) from the "Actions" section.
- o Finally, after performing a computation, the "Summarize" tool will output the data to a new column based on the name that's listed in the "Output Field Name" column in the "Actions" section.
  - ▪ You can accept the default name of the new column, rename it in the "Summarize" tool's "Output Field Name," or rename the column later in the workflow with a "Select" tool (my preferred method for reasons outlined in previous chapters).

Field	Action	Output Field Name
Sales Price	Sum ▼	Sum_Sales Price

How to sum data using the "Summarize" tool

- Now that you've got a handle on how to configure the "Summarize" tool, let's use it to sum our sales data.

- To do this, click on the "Sales Price" line in the "Fields" section of the configuration.

- Now click on the "Add" button in the "Actions" section.
  - o From here, you'll see a dropdown menu with numerous computation options.
  - o After selecting "Sum," the "Actions" section of the configuration will look like what's pictured.

Fields:

	Field	Type
	Transaction Date	Date
	Product	V_String
▶	Sales Price	Double
	Credit Card	V_String
	Country	V_String
	State	V_String
	City	V_String
	Date Account Cr...	DateTime
	Last Login	DateTime

Add ▼

- When you run the workflow, Alteryx will create a new column called "Sum_Sales Price" (see the "Output Field Name"), and the total sales will be shown as pictured in the illustration that follows.

Actions:

	Field	Action	Output Field Name
▶	Sales Price	Sum ▼	Sum_Sales Price

	Sum_Sales Price
1	1612500

An example of using the "Summarize" tool to break down sales into various categories

- While we see from the example above that we can use Alteryx to verify total sales in our Excel file, that's not very helpful in and of itself.
  - After all, we can already quickly, easily, and reliably sum large groups of figures using Excel; we don't need Alteryx for that.

- One way Alteryx can add value is to automatically break sales down by various categories.

- For example, let's say that we need to break sales down by U.S. state.
  - This could be useful for sales and marketing purposes.
  - This is also necessary for state income tax calculations.

- As a first step, we "Add" the field "State" to the "Actions" section of the "Summarize" tool's configuration and select "Group By."
  - We also use the up-arrow to move "State" above "Sales Price" because we FIRST want to group our data by state and then we want to see the sales by state.
  - Following is what this looks like in the "Summarize" tool's configuration.

Actions: **Add** ▼

	Field	Action	Output Field Name
▶	State	Group By ▼	State
	Sales Price	Sum ▼	Sum_Sales Price

↑ ↓ ⊖

- After running the workflow, a (partial) preview of our output is as follows.

	State	Sum_Sales Price
1	[Null]	13200
2	AK	8400
3	AL	3600
4	AR	9900
5	AZ	16850
6	Aargau	3600
7	Abu Zaby	1200
8	Al Manamah	1200
9	Alberta	26400
10	Alsace	1200

- We can immediately make a few of observations.
  - First, we have some "nowhere sales" to deal with in our dataset (the $13,200 on the first row in the table at the bottom of the previous page).
    - However, the amount is relatively small compared to total sales of $1,612,500.
    - As a result, if we can't immediately find the location for these "nowhere sales," we can likely ignore this amount or allocate it among all states on a pro rata basis.
  - The bigger problem, however, is that sales to foreign territories (such as Canadian provinces) are also in the "State" column of our data.
  - Thus, to get U.S.-only sales, this is an issue we're going to have to address.

- To do so, we recognize that we _first_ need to organize the data by _country_, then by state, and then by sales according to this configuration.

Field	Action	Output Field Name
Country	Group By	Country
State	Group By	State
Sales Price	Sum	Sum_Sales Price

- After running the workflow, a (partial) preview of our output is as follows.

	Country	State	Sum_Sales Price
1	Argentina	Buenos Aires	1200
2	Australia	New South Wales	20400
3	Australia	Queensland	13200
4	Australia	South Australia	1200
5	Australia	Tasmania	3600
6	Australia	Victoria	13200
7	Australia	Western Australia	12000
8	Austria	Lower Austria	2400
9	Austria	Tyrol	3600
10	Austria	Vienna	4800
11	Bahrain	Al Manamah	1200
12	Belgium	Antwerpen	1200
13	Belgium	Brussels (Bruxelles)	9600

- This is an improvement in that we've now stratified "State" data by country. However, we've now got foreign country data mixed in with US data.
  - How can we fix this? How do we keep ROWS that we want in our data and "filter" out the ones that we want to remove?
  - Correct...this sounds like a job for the "Filter" tool.
  - That being the case, we add it to our workflow after the "Summarize" tool as show below.

Clean Sales
Data.xlsx
Table=`Sheet1$`

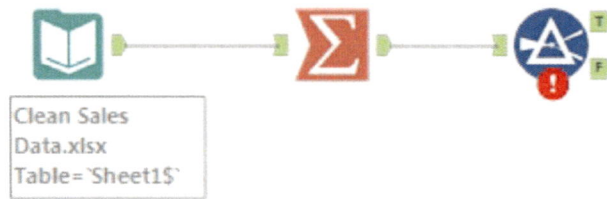

- The exclamation point indicates that we need to configure the "Filter," too, and we do so as follows.

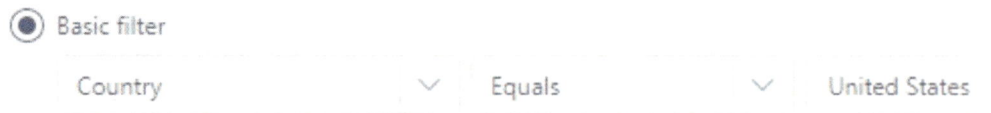

⦿ Basic filter

| Country | ∨ | Equals | ∨ | United States |

- After running the workflow, a (partial) preview of our output from the "Filter" tool's "T" (or "True") output anchor is as follows.

[This space was intentionally left blank].

	Country	State	Sum_Sales Price
1	United States	AK	8400
2	United States	AL	3600
3	United States	AR	9900
4	United States	AZ	16850
5	United States	CA	112150
6	United States	CO	27400
7	United States	CT	10800
8	United States	DC	6000
9	United States	DE	1200
10	United States	FL	51600

- After using the "Select" tool to remove the "Country" column and to rename "Sum_Sales_Price," our output looks like this.

	State	Sales by State
1	AK	8400
2	AL	3600
3	AR	9900
4	AZ	16850
5	CA	112150
6	CO	27400
7	CT	10800
8	DC	6000
9	DE	1200
10	FL	51600

- In summary, by logically grouping fields (columns) in the "Summarize" tool's "Action" section, and by combining "Summarize" tool's capabilities with other tools, you can *dramatically* increase the transparency and the usefulness of your data. [36]

12.5 The "Summarize" Tool's "Group by" Action is a Powerful way to Aggregate Data in Rows

- I've previously explained and illustrated numerous times (including in the last section) that the "Filter" tool is an excellent way to manage rows.

- However, the "Filter" tool has limitations.
    - An obvious one is that it organizes data by REMOVING rows so that what you need is all that remains.
    - But how do you organize rows when you need ALL of your data for your output to be complete and accurate?
    - For example, consider the following snapshot from our sales data.

	Transaction Date	Product	Sales Price	Credit Card	Country	State
39	2009-01-09	Product1	1200	Mastercard	United States	TX
40	2009-01-06	Product2	3600	Amex	United States	VT
41	2009-01-06	Product2	3600	Amex	United States	VT
42	2009-01-07	Product1	1200	Mastercard	United States	GA
43	2009-01-03	Product1	1200	Visa	Denmark	Frederiksborg
44	2009-01-07	Product2	3600	Visa	United States	IL
45	2009-01-07	Product1	1200	Amex	United States	TX

- How would we use the *"Filter"* tool (vs. the "Summarize" tool) to determine sales by state?
    - While it's possible to *eventually* compute sales by state using the "Filter" tool, it would be a terribly inefficient choice.
        - For example, you would first have to filter out Texas sales and sum those, then Vermont and sum those, and so on for the rest of the states.
        - Afterwards you would need to aggregate that data in one source before exporting it to Excel. Ugh. ☹
        - Fortunately, as shown in the previous example, using the "Summarize" tool is an extremely efficient way to do this.

- In fact, the "Summarize" tool's "Group By" capability is so powerful for organizing data in rows that I want to drive the point home with another example.

---

[36] If needed (for sales tax purposes, for example), you could follow the same methodology as outlined in this example to determine sales by city. In short, you can get sales data as granular as you need it based on the data available.

- Take another look at the final output of the sales by state example in the illustration to the right.

- Do you see the significance of what we accomplished from a grouping/data aggregation standpoint?

- The answer is:
  - We used the "Summarize" tool to take state-related sales data that was previously on MANY rows and
  - We aggregated (or collapsed) that data so that sales for *each state* are condensed to a *single line*.

	State	Sales by State
1	AK	8400
2	AL	3600
3	AR	9900
4	AZ	16850
5	CA	112150
6	CO	27400
7	CT	10800
8	DC	6000
9	DE	1200
10	FL	51600

- Does this example help you to see the possibilities for using the "Summarize" tool for managing data organized in rows?!
  - As another example, what if we wanted see sales aggregated by credit card type?
  - To do so, we would use the following configuration in the "Summarize" tool.

Field	Action	Output Field Name
Credit Card	Group By ▼	Credit Card
Sales Price	Sum ▼	Sum_Sales Price

- After running the workflow, the output would look like this.

	Credit Card	Sum_Sales Price
1	Amex	188900
2	Diners	129000
3	Mastercard	454850
4	Visa	839750

- We could go on and on – there is almost no limit to the possibilities. The key is to understand that the "Summarize" tool's "Group By" capability is an extremely quick, effective, and accurate way to aggregate data organized in rows.

12.6 The "Summarize" Tool Also Counts Data and Can Perform Other Type of Analysis

- The "Summarize" tool is very flexible in that it contains numerous options to calculate, organize and summarize data.

- For example, using our same sales dataset, what if we wanted to know how many products were sold by product category?
  - To find out, we would configure the "Summarize" tool as follows.

Field	Action		Output Field Name
Product	Group By	▼	Product
Product	Count	▼	Count

- Before looking at the output, here are few things we have not encountered before.
  - We are analyzing the SAME column twice ("Product").
    - First, the "Group By" breaks out product data by product type.
    - Second, we're using a new action, "Count," to determine the number of products that were sold in each category.

- After running the workflow, the output looks like this.

	Product	Count
1	Product1	835
2	Product2	135
3	Product3	15

- There are numerous other ways you can use the "Summarize" tool to organize, compute and to summarize your data. To name just a few that are meaningful to accounting, tax, and finance professionals, you can:
  - Average values.
  - Find the minimum or maximum value in a dataset.
  - Count empty (or null) and non-null data.

12.7 The "Summarize" tool and Internal Controls ("SOX") Considerations

Alteryx and internal controls

- I previously made it clear that I believe that Excel is the best, most flexible tool for documenting internal controls and proving out the related calculations.

- HOWEVER, this doesn't just happen by itself. After all, Excel starts out as a "blank piece of paper;" meaning an Excel workbook only contains what you put into it (whether your data or work product is good OR bad).

- But again, it's precisely that fact that Excel is a blank slate that enables you to easily show and reference your work in a way that meets specific SOX/internal controls needs.

- That said, there is much that can be done within Alteryx to improve a workflow's "reviewability", thus enabling you to take advantage of Designer's power while maintaining (and even enhancing) internal controls.

An example of internal (or SOX) controls documentation in Alteryx

- Using the techniques we've covered in this chapter, assume that we've used the "Summarize" tool to distill our data down to sales by product category for financial accounting computations.

	Product	Sum_Sales Price
1	Product1	1014000
2	Product2	486000
3	Product3	112500

- The good news is that we were able to accomplish this quickly and easily.
  - But then there's the question, how do we get a reviewer comfortable that our output is correct?
  - One way would be to use the "Comment" tool to add descriptions to the following workflow.[37]

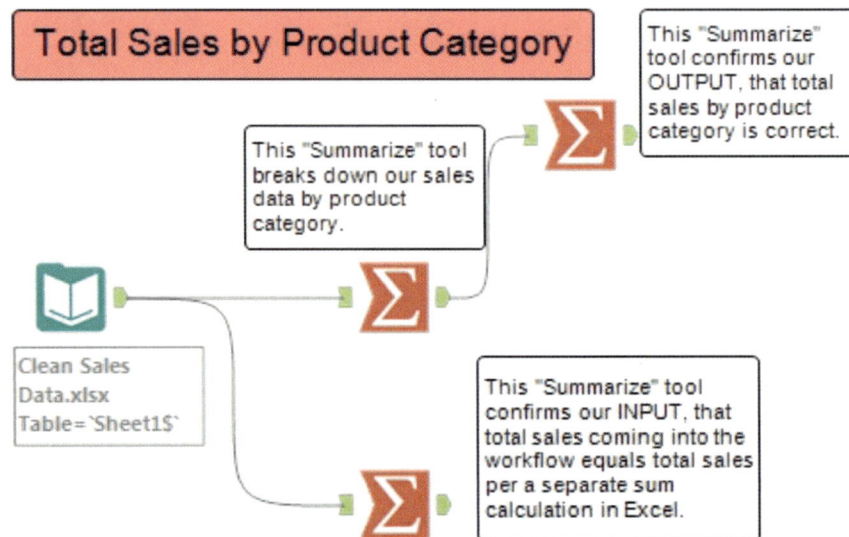

- Based on the descriptions in the example above, we developed our internal controls based on the following rationale.

---

[37] For information, I used the "Comment" tool to add the notes to the workflow above.

1) In Excel, we summed total sales in the "Clean Sales Data" workbook prior to importing it into Alteryx.
   a. After doing do, we saw that total sales per the raw data was $1,612,500.

2) We imported the raw Excel data into the workflow.
   a. This is represented by the "Input Data" tool at the beginning of the workflow shown on the previous page.

3) We then connected the "Summarize" tool pictured at the bottom of the workflow (the third one down).
   a. The purpose of this "Summarize" tool is to calculate the total sales per the data in the "Input Data" tool.
   b. In doing so, we saw that it's $1,612,500.
   c. This is exactly same total we computed in Excel, so we've confirmed that the sales data coming into the workflow is accurate.

Sum_Sales Price
1 1612500

4) Next, we placed the "Summarize" tool in the middle of the workflow. It's here that we computed the sales breakdown by product category.
   a. While the sales by product breakdown displayed to the right is great, it reveals a shortcoming of Alteryx. Namely, the "Summarize" tool doesn't display a TOTAL in the sales column.

	Product	Sum_Sales Price
1	Product1	1014000
2	Product2	486000
3	Product3	112500

5) To compensate for this, we added the final "Summarize" tool at the top of the workflow.
   a. We used this tool to sum total sales for products.
   b. This amount is $1,612,500, which is equal to the total sales coming into the workflow per the Excel file.

Sum_Sales Price
1 1612500

- In summary, by following the steps above, we've proven that our sales data ties out in total at the beginning and the end of our workflow.
  o This provides strong internal controls support that our sales by product breakdown is complete and accurate.

Use the "Comments" tool to document your process within Alteryx

- Some of the first questions a reviewer will ask when evaluating your work are, "What am I looking at," "How is the calculation flowing," and "Why does it matter?"

Comment

- These questions can be addressed using the "Comments" tool, as illustrated in the previous example.
  o There we added a title to the workflow, clearly stating its purpose ("Total Sales by Product Category").

- o We also added comments boxes at key junctures in the workflow to explain what actions were being performed and why.

- In summary, the "Comments" tool is extremely simple and effective way to document SOX controls, and these same principles can be applied to add robust documentation to much larger and more complex workflows than the one shown in our previous example.[38]

---

[38] Based on my observations and experience, the "Comments" tool is VASTLY underestimated, underappreciated, and underutilized.

13 Parting Thoughts

13.1 Alteryx and Excel Make a Great Team

- It should be abundantly clear by now, but I think it's worth repeating now that we've come to the end of this book:

I believe Excel and Alteryx are <u>both</u> powerful tools that are made even more powerful when <u>used together</u>.

13.2 Become Self-Sufficient Where Possible in Obtaining Source Data

- We've assumed throughout this material that we've had access to source data, almost like it feel out of the sky.

- As accounting, tax and financial professionals with any experience know, it's *rare* in practice to be able to obtain and access the data and information you need without sustained, intentional effort on your part.

- You will *greatly* enhance your professional effectiveness using Alteryx (or doing anything else for that matter) if you learn to become *self-sufficient* in obtaining data. Examples include:
    - Extracting accounting data directly from your organization's ERP system.
    - Running reports using your tax provision and compliance software.
    - Downloading data directly from a website, etc.

- The alternative to accessing data on your own is begging for it, waiting for it, stressing over it, and wasting time in the process.
    - Accounting will get it for you "after the quarter close."
    - Your client will send it "soon."
    - HR will get you that report "after they finish up performance reviews."
    - Tax will get back to you "after their deadline."
        - By the way, did you know that tax has "deadlines" throughout the year?!

- Other positive benefits of obtaining data on your own are:
    - It will increase your job satisfaction, because it puts planning when you do your work more within your control.
    - You will be able to more reliably predict how long it will take you to complete your assignments.

- It increases your credibility when others know you can directly access the facts needed to:
  - Produce deliverables and
  - Provide the factual support necessary to make informed decisions.

- In summary, learn how to obtain source data on your own in every way possible. As you do, you'll dramatically improve your performance in terms of speed and effectiveness.

13.3 NASBA Compliant Alteryx CPE

If you would to enroll in NASBA compliant CPE I've produced on Alteryx, then see:

- www.nctaxdirector.com/courses or
- taxdirectorservices.advancecpe.com.

Made in the USA
Las Vegas, NV
21 May 2024